Pewter
Through five hundred years

Studio Vista
Christie's

Pewter
Through five hundred years

Gabriele Sterner

Christie's South Kensington Collectors' Guides

A production of Plenary
Publications International, Amsterdam

Series editor: Albrecht Bangert
Design: Joerk Reitz
Translation: Roland Matthews

A Studio Vista book published
by Cassell Ltd,
35 Red Lion Square, London, WC1R 4SG
and at Sydney, Auckland, Toronto, Johannesburg,
an affiliate of
Macmillan Publishing Co., Inc., New York

ISBN 0-289-708702
Filmset in Great Britain by TNR Productions, London
Printed and bound by Grijelmo, S.A., Bilbao, Spain

Contents

Collecting Pewter

Pewter is a material which is enjoying increasing popularity and recognition, having for long stood in the shadow of the precious metal silver. The forms of old pewter have stood the test of time, maturing over the centuries; with the air of peace and comfort which they convey and the soft gleam of their surfaces, they complement the more obvious necessities of modern home decor, and can stimulate a real delight in collecting.

Tin has played an important role in mankind's cultural development. Alloying it with copper made possible the manufacture of bronze at a very early date in human history, although there is scant literary evidence for the use of tin in the production of the vessels and implements of antiquity (and such as there is is not always completely clear). Only a few vessels and statuettes have been preserved, pewter being highly susceptible to weathering. Excavations in the 18th and 19th centuries brought to light clay vessels and clay figures with little pieces of pewter inlay; these have been dated to the Late Stone Age or the succeeding Bronze Age.

Amulets found in many graves in Upper Egypt have a high lead content; they are considered to be the work of Coptic Christians between the 4th and 7th centuries AD. Pewterware from the Roman epoch has been found in Britain: the tin used in it possibly came from Cornish mines.

The importance of pewter as a material in the early Middle Ages is attested by Theophilus Presbyter's *Schedula diversarum artium* (c. 1100), which includes a detailed description of all the processes involved in the manufacture of pewter hollow-ware: nothing, however, has been preserved from these early times. It was soon after the tin-mines at Erzgebirge, on the borders of Saxony and Bohemia, were first worked, that the local population gradually set about substituting the more durable pewter for the wood and clay which had previously furnished their tableware.

The large quantities of tin reaching Europe from the East Indies at the end of the 15th century pushed prices down and gave pewter art its first major impetus. Whereas in the early Middle Ages the pewterer's craft stood mainly at the service of

Portrait of the merchant Georg Gisze, oak, 96 × 85.7 cm; Hans Holbein the younger 1497–1543. Gemaldegalerie Berlin (West), Stattliche Museen Preussischer Kulturbesitz. On the table can be seen a pewter coin-box and a pewter beaker.

the church, in the late Middle Ages the demand for pewter objects and ornaments was growing in lay circles too; thus we find not only a great variety of good solid tableware but also magnificient flagons, tankards, dishes and other showpieces which adorned the sumptuous tables and sideboards of the day.

By the middle of the 14th century the pewter trade was well established in this country: 'Ordinances' for a Craft of Pewterers are known, dated 1348. The first Royal Charter was granted to the Pewterers' Company (as it became known) in 1473. Unfortunately much of the early pewter collected in their Hall in Lime Street was destroyed with the Hall in the Great Fire of London in 1666.

Good examples of early guild pewter can still be found in Europe, particularly in Germany, where many guilds used pewterware for their craft shields and ceremonial objects.

The late Renaissance produced a new feature which had very important consequences for the artistic development of pewter: for the first time pewter objects were made to serve no practical function but simply to be admired as showpieces. These are known as 'display pewter' to distinguish them from everyday pewter; in terms of treatment and style they resemble

Views of an old pewterer's workshop, reconstructed in the Weygang Museum, Ohringen.

silverwork, although they have relief decoration cast in the mould, rather than engraved.

The basic forms that are found in the Renaissance recur in the Baroque period. With Rococo pewter we find an even stronger imitation of silverwork together with a gradual decrease in the use of the metal in favour of porcelain, faience and even earthenware. With the advent of Neoclassicism around 1800 the freer lines of the past give way to strict ornamental bands of acanthus leaves, oak wreaths, strings of pearls or festoons, picked out in bas-relief. Among the objects of this period to have survived are numerous salts of filigree design (many with coloured-glass insets) as well as candlesticks and claw-foot sugar-bowls. The mid-19th century in Europe enhanced the reputation of pewter, for Historicism, with its love of traditional styles, gave rise to frequent copies of old forms. At the turn of this century, the artists of Art Nouveau performed wonders in the casting and cutting of pewter; with great skill they made patterns of flowers and animals emerge from the smooth surface of the metal. Finally, in our own century we find efforts being made to rediscover the intrinsic beauty of

Three medieval Hanseatic flagons. The Hanseatic flagon is a North German flagon type of the 14th to 16th centuries, deriving its name from its used throughout the Hansa's sphere of influence. These flagons are always pear-shaped and compact in appearance, the lower part of the body being sharply drawn in. They have flat lids and double-acorn or double-ball thumb-pieces on the hinge. The sturdy handle is S-shaped and often carries relief work. Hanseatic flagons were used both as pouring vessels and as drinking vessels, the oldest surviving examples dating from the first half of the 14th century. They have mainly been salvaged from shipwrecks and other underwater sites. Unmarked. North German. 14th-15th cent. Heights: 20 – 34 cm.

pewter in the simple, unadorned forms which traditional British pewterware had always followed. As early as the 19th century there was a keen demand for antique pewter, and it could hardly be satisfied by the small amount of good material available. Enterprising pewterers were quick to recognise the rewards to be reaped; the result was a large number of imitations and fakes (some, admittedly, of good quality). Another factor which increases the difficulties faced by the collector seeking out significant and valuable items is the natural decrease in the number of pewter pieces caused by the wear and tear of time.

For the enthusiastic collector as much as for the committed expert, the most important thing is to *grasp* pewter, in all senses of the word. An eye for quality and originality needs to be trained, as does the ability to sense the value of a given piece. A serious interest in pewter, and above all this ability to *grasp* through observation and comparison, will lead to a 'feel' for the genuine article. In addition the collector will require not only a considerable knowledge of the subject itself but also some acquaintance with the relevant cultural background.

In this book an attempt has been made to arrange the different aspects of pewter in such a way as to give a clear survey, while at the same time taking account of a whole range of special interests. In order to avoid presenting the wealth of material in a dry, factual way, the individual chapters have been arranged not simply according to country or period, but more according to the various areas in which pewter has been used. In addition the enthusiast will find a comprehensive bibliography as well as practical hints on starting and building a collection. The question of fakes, of such importance to the collector, is discussed at length; and advice is given on the care and maintenance of pewter.

It has been the author's concern and desire to present pewter wares not as isolated *objets d'art*, but as living testimonies to the ages that produced them.

Der Kandelgiesser ('The Pewterer') Jost Amman, showing the craftsman and his booth. Frankfurt am Main 1568.

The Living Past

The history of pewter is at the same time a history of the social habits of our ancestors and, as such, a frequent source of entertainment and instruction. Most of those objects that were once the pride of every table have suffered the same fate as their companions, the revellers of past centuries who have long since turned to dust; what little has been left us is the more to be treasured. Being in everyday use and susceptible to changes in fashion, household pewter has been subject, naturally enough, to wear and tear; in addition there have been times when it has been considered necessary to melt the metal down and recast it as coinage, or for war.

Medieval Table Customs

In the Middle Ages vast quantities of food were consumed and similar amounts drunk. A feast for Richard II included, for example, four different soups as well as roast pork, pheasant, chicken and venison together with quail, lark, heron and cranes. Not surprisingly such a meal would be washed down with ypocras, a mulled wine infused with spices, which was thought to

have salutary digestive properties! And one medieval recipe for ypocras specifies pewter vessels for the infusion: they should hold about a gallon each. Unbridled intemperance was at times almost considered a virtue, which helps to explain the evolution of different kinds of drinking bout around a central code of conduct.

The most widespread of drinking customs was that of drinking a person's health; it was also the source of the greatest indignation in sermons. Anyone refusing to answer a toast was considered to have committed a severe breach of honour and would usually have to reckon with bloody consequences. By the end of the 15th century this custom had grown to such an extent that counter-measures were invoked: rulers imposed bans, the church thundered from the pulpit, and books appeared 'opposing the demon drink'. Temperance societies were formed at the beginning of the 16th century, and the threat posed by drinking was even debated in Germany at Imperial Diets. The reminiscences of the knight Hans von Schweinichen, with their constant and contented refrain of 'got nicely drunk again today', give an accurate and

Wine pitcher. Cylindrical body, in the middle of which there is a bas-relief frieze of lozenges, engraved with flowers and owner's mark. The German inscription reads in translation: 'The two brothers Hermann Huge and Jurgen Huge have had this pitcher repaired for their grandfather Johann Huge in the year 1674'. On the lip a hexagonal wheel. Unmarked. Height: 29.5 cm. The lid is new and bears a relief medallion depicting three *Landsknechte* (mercenary foot-soldiers). Marked I H P, Munich. On the lozenge is the initial F.

expression in the range and richness of the vessels used, and it was pewter vessels, more than any others, which enjoyed the greatest popularity, a popularity which lasted many centuries, thanks to their toughness, so vital a prerequisite of the practices of the taproom. There were traditional beaker forms, but beyond these there was no limit to the makers' fantasy and innovative powers. The growing pleasure taken in drinking in the 16th century unleashed a constant stream of ideas for new types of drinking vessel.

The more grotesque, indeed the more obscene the vessel, the happier someone was to drink from it: German pewterers of the 17th century displayed particular ingenuity in this field.

In all cultures and at all times drinking has enjoyed an importance commensurate with eating. It cannot be denied, however, that the inhabitants of the cooler climes of northern Europe have been especially thirsty people. Thus the French word for 'drinking a toast' is *trinquer*: apparently, the French identified the clinking of glasses, previously unknown to them, with the act of drinking itself, and hence derived the word *trinquer* from the German *trinken* (meaning simply 'to drink'). The drinking culture found visual expression in the wealth and variety of its drinking vessels,

representative picture of life at that time. Another knight, Shakespeare's comic hero Sir John Falstaff, also showed a fondness for wine that one can be sure was shared by his live contemporaries. The drinking cult found visual

above Lidded tankard. On the lid 'wriggled work' and engraved coat of arms; on the drum the inscription: Ich bring dem Herren ein guten Trunk ('I bring the gentlemen a good drink'). Marks of Breslau and the date 1615 on the lid. Height: 14.5 cm.

above left Rorken or Wein-Kross are typical North German drinking vessels of the 17th and 18th centuries. The Glucksrorken ('lucky' Rorken) have hollow piercework feet containing little dice.

below left Deckelschoppen are tankards or drinking mugs. Deckelschoppen of the Blacksmiths' Company, marked 1821, Georg Chr. Gottfr. Druhl, Hamburg, master 1812. Deckelschoppen of the Carpenters' company, marked 1886, no stamp. Deckelschoppen of the Sail-makers, marked 1794, Carl Georg Buttner, Altona, master 1781. Tankard of the Knackers, marked 1672, Christoffer Harmann, Hamburg, master 1659. Deckelschoppen of the Shipbuilding Day-labourers, mid-18th century, Gottlieb Leberecht Kraeft I, Altona, master 1756. Heights: 25 – 16 cm.

above Two engraved tankards. Left; tankard with inscription Durch Einigkeit bestandig (cf. 'In unity is strength'). Marked 1842, Klaus Christian Wolters, Hamburg. Right; tankard, marked 1761, probably Danish, no stamp. Heights: 25 – 20 cm.

below Beakers are drinking vessels without lids or handles: Carpenters' beaker, marked 1730, Hinnrich Brumer the Younger, Hamburg; Two Locksmiths' beakers, c.1815. Lathe-turners' beaker, marked 1865, Bartels. Beaker of the Basket-weavers' company, marked 1778, Georg Matt. Grave, Hamburg. Three beakers of the Potters' company, marked 1811. Beaker of the Cole-seed Threshers, marked 1816. Friendship beaker, marked 1848. Heights: 18 – 8 cm.

Detail of a
wine pitcher.
Mid-17th century.
Notice how the
lid-hinge has been
cast separately.
The maker's mark
is on the inner side
of the handle.

Wine pitcher.
Flat-lidded, hoop-
handle with
foliage ornament.
Early, 18th century,
French Switzerland,
Francesco Felice
Rovero. On the
leaf-shaped lid the
initials MM and
three marks.
Height: 37.5 cm.

which were later found all over
Europe.

Drinking and Pouring Vessels

A description of household pewter
must take as its point of departure
the medieval period. For time
limits cannot be drawn, not at least
on the basis of typology, since the
characteristic forms that were
already emerging in the 15th
century did not undergo significant
changes in the succeeding centuries,
but tended to retain certain
distinguishing features.

Pots and Flagons

Good examples of the oldest

surviving pewter objects are the so-
called 'Hanseatic flagons' which
were found during building
excavations and are now on display
in the Historical Museum of the
City of Hamburg. These vessels, all
with lids, have a massive solidity
which contrasts with their modest
form. The underside of the lid or
the bottom of the tankard itself is
often decorated with a tin plaque
showing Christ on the Cross or the
Madonna and Child. This form
occurs also in the Netherlands,
Scandinavia, Brandenburg and the
Lower Rhine - in other words, in
the Hansa's sphere of influence;
hence the name. (The Hansa or
Hanseatic League had started
around 1280 as an alliance of
merchants, but after 1356 was a

league of towns).

This type of vessel, which was used not only for pouring but also for drinking, is recorded as early as the beginning of the 14th century. Its rough functionalism is characteristic of the medieval period; the body of the vessel is drawn in tightly at the neck to give it the shape of a pear, and it rests on a conical base. A flat lid covers the broad neck with its everted lip, while the hinge has a double-ball or double-acorn thumbpiece. The sturdy handle is often S-shaped, with foliage decoration. This design can be compared to what is believed to be the earliest surviving English flagon, formerly used in the church at Woodeaton in Oxfordshire, and now in the collection of the Worshipful Company of Pewterers. It can be dated to the latter part of Elizabeth I's reign, and has an S-shaped handle, a bulbous body on a raised foot and a domed lid with finial.

An example of a more capacious type is provided by the 'Bossian flagon', so called because the oldest surviving example of this type, dating from the early 16th century, bears the mark of the Dutch town Hertogenbosch. One characteristic feature of these small pear-shaped pots is the footring, whose sides rise vertically, then taper off into a sudden bend. The base is as tall as the body itself,

and the whole vessel is no more than eleven to fifteen centimetres high - a clear indication that pots were also used as drinking vessels, especially as toasting cups. For any guest, on entering a house, would be handed the toasting cup, which he then had to drain.

Before discussing the various forms pewter could traditionally take, it is best to look briefly at a most important aspect of early pewter, namely its use for ecclesiastical objects. Many of the earliest surviving pieces of pewter are chalices, tazzas or patens, often with an inscription in commemoration of the donor. In some cases it appears that the piece was made for secular purposes and later given to the church. Though many such pieces were most probably destroyed in the Cromwellian era, some still survive in parish churches, cathedrals and museums.

Drinking Vessels

Drinking vessels were not generally handled with the greatest delicacy; this explains the many dents and scratches found on them, which are perfectly understandable marks of wear and tear. One of the consequences of their use was that drinking vessels were often engraved with the owner's name or monogram to prevent confusion.

The most popular of all drinking vessels was without doubt the

A fine example of an English flagon of the Cromwellian era. 9½ inches high.

tankard or mug, although it is not always easy to distinguish it in form from a flagon. The shape and style of the mug, and above all the design and decoration of the thumbpiece, served to indicate the social and financial status of the owner. Mugs, like pots, evolved their own elaborate typology. The simplest drinking vessel was the beaker; it had the form of a truncated cylindrical cone, with or without a handle. Some variants of this basic form were also produced in the Middle Ages. If he so wished, the owner could have his initials or crest as decoration as

well as to indicate ownership. Sometimes a stamp was added, not unlike a pewtérer's touch; in many cases this was the only decoration on the piece. In England, relief decoration on early pieces is rare, but 'wriggled work' is found on tankards and porringers. Such designs have a charming simplicity about them.

Stave Mugs, Faience Mugs, Apostle Mugs

As the broad mass of the population endeavoured to emulate the habits of the upper classes, especially from the early 16th century onwards, so household wares came increasingly to serve a double function, as useful (and used) items, and as ornaments. If purses did not extend to gold or silver tableware, at least pewterware could be decorated with other materials. Stave mugs and faience mugs are European examples of this trend.

The traditional German 'beer mug' with a pewter lid and rim on a base made of gaudily decorated earthenware is well known, though such mixtures of materials are not found in English work. A less well known German mug (illustrated on page 22) is the apostle mug. The old custom of *Minnetrinken* (toasting absent or dead friends) became extended into drinking to the memory of the Apostles or the

Stave mug, known since 1929 as a 'Lichtenhain tankard'. The wooden staves are mounted in pewter and decorated with pewter inlay. The beaked mug, which can be locked, is adorned with vine-leaves and fitted with two handles, enabling it to be used as both a drinking and a pouring vessel. Stave pots come mainly from the area between Kulmbach and Hof, where around forty are known to have been produced in the 18th century. This particularly fine example probably dates from around 1740; it carries three unidentified marks. Height: 27 cm.

Detail of above. Notice the intricate working of the hinge, and the pewter inlaid into the wood.

saints: a custom apparently originated by Otto the Great when he visited the monastery of St. Emmeran. Many German tankards had in their base a filter known as a 'nutmeg cup', which could be unscrewed and filled with spices; in this way, the drinker could satisfy his own taste in mulled ale or wine. The medallion set into the base of the filter might be a rosette, or else contain a figured relief, for example a Crucifixion group, a Madonna and Child, the Agnus Dei or a municipal coat of arms. Similar medallions are found in the bases of some English baluster measures. The pewter tankard is one of the most common forms of English pewterware: indeed pewter pint and half-pint pots are still common sights in pubs, either as decoration or in use! From the collector's point of view, the tankards of the Stuart period are considered among the most sought-after. Such tankards have a fairly squat cylindrical shape, with little taper, and a flat hinged lid. The drum might have wriggled work engraving on it, but would more often be plain, and about 4 or 5 inches deep. The lid would be surmounted by an elaborate thumb-piece. Various designs for thumb-pieces are known, such as ramshorn, bombe, palm tree or love-birds. After about 1685, tankards began to be made with domed lids, and the plain drum often carried a

single band or 'fillet' about a third of the way up. This shape remained popular until the end of the 18th century, when lidded tankards became less common. The designs for English flagons resemble those of early tankards, save that flagons are considerably deeper: examples up to a foot from base to lip are known, though nine inches is a commoner height. The lids of flagons were normally domed, however, rather than flat, though one type was called a Beefeater flagon, as the lid resembled the traditional Beefeater's hat. Unlike tankards, flagons could be for secular or sacramental use. By the time of Queen Anne, the simple ramshorn thumbpiece had become more scrolled and elaborate: the term 'chairback' is often used to describe this shape.

Mug. Breslau, dated 1774.

Two English tankards. The left hand one is unlidded and has characteristically plain lines. The other has a domed lid, ball finial to the handle and an engraved coat design on the front side. Note also the reeding on the body.

Lidless 'tavern pots' were made from the end of the 17th century onwards: the bodies are not so short as on tankards, and taper more sharply. Often the pewterer would supply the innkeeper with a wooden plug to match the tankards' shape, so as to help straightening them out. Another development during the 18th century was the tulip-shaped tankard, with the drum curved in towards the base and widening at the top. This shape was also found unlidded. At the same time the shape and decoration of handles became more inventive, the plain ball finial giving way to fishtail and double volute shapes.

Eating Utensils and Tableware

Bricklayers' mug. Silesia, dated 1650.

The quantity and quality of the tableware in a private household was determined by the host's financial standing; he saw it as a

Apostle mug. Stoneware with pewter mounts, glazed colour-painting on brown-glaze base. The twelve apostles and their attributes are depicted in the midst of floral patterns. The painter's mark M has not been identified. The pewter casing dates from the 19th century. The lid has a ball-shaped thumb-piece and is very finely moulded; it depicts Justice with a frieze reading Justitia et Pietas constans animusque triumphant. No discernible marks. Height: 21 cm. The combination of stoneware and pewter is found especially in beer-mugs and has been very popular since the 17th century.

way in which he could show off his home to good effect and honour his guests. The various drinking vessels and pouring vessels naturally enough attracted the attention of the guests, but there were also sauce-boats, spice-jars, salts and plates to enhance the lavish impression afforded by the host's table. A list of household effects made in 1514 testifies already to a solid prosperity:

'Pewter dishes and platters, large and small, sauceboats and mixing pots, silver beakers and golden casks; porringers and bowls and many a strange glass - square, pointed, tall, narrow and wide; and whatever one needs by way of cans and bottles, large and small.'

The well-to-do middle classes were able to afford a certain amount of silver tableware by this time, although pewter continued in most cases to do service for everyday purposes. Pewter, together with copper, was the tableware material most favoured by the artisan class

Drinking cups in the form of a 'Gretchen pot'. Two handles shaped as the heads of female herms. Finely wrought rosette in the well. Illegible marking. c.1900. Height: 18 cm.

in general in the 16th century, even though wooden wares continued to figure prominently. Pewterware gleamed equally in the burgher's smart kitchen and on the dressers, chests and mantelpieces of the peasant's cottage.

Plates and Dishes

Liquid foods were eaten from flat dishes, bowls, or porringers, which were mainly of pewter (although wood and clay were also found in poorer households). They do not seem to have been consigned to any particular use; the liquid was picked up as one wished, either with a spoon or by dunking bread. There was no guarantee, however, that a guest would even have such a bowl to himself. Erasmus's oft-quoted 'Rules of the Table' tell us that two guests should share a single utensil, and especially a drinking vessel. Whether such eating in pairs meant in fact a man

and a woman remains unclear. This custom of eating in pairs originated in France and had been very popular since the 12th century, when notions of chivalry became such an important feature of courtly life. Previously the custom had been that men and women ate at separate tables, or else the men ate alone, while the women served. This practice left its mark; for example, the hostess would herself serve a specially honoured guest, as is described in such medieval epics as *Parsifal* and *Tristan*.

An English plate, with wriggled work decoration, in the form of a spray of flowers surmounted by the owner's initials and with the dates of his birth and (probably) marriage, for such plates were often made in pairs, one for the bride and one for the groom.

The plate

The plate can be formally described as an eating utensil, circular in shape, flatter than a dish, and normally no more than ten inches across. No pewter plates have been preserved from medieval times, doubtless because they were

Pewter covers with owners' initials and markings. 18th century.

Pear-shaped mug. Faience, with pewter footring and pewter lid bearing a mask. Unmarked. Height: 23 cm.

Faience beer-mug, decorated with a cartouche depicting a putto with skull and hourglass. No painter's mark. Pewter mounts also unmarked. On the lid a medallion engraved with the initials EMH and the date 1761. Height: 24 cm.

Faience beer-mug, decorated with a bouquet of flowers; the painter's mark features a fish and the initials POPP. The pewter mounts, base and lid have two marks, one of which is a 'fine metal' mark showing the date 1760, the Wurttemberg antlers, and a dice with five points and the figure 5 beneath. Height: 24 cm.

the easiest forms to melt down. We can, however, understand how they looked from paintings of the 14th and 15th centuries, as well as from contemporary descriptions. Initially they were simply round, flat discs, which gradually evolved a narrow raised rim. In the 16th century the well of the plate grew smaller and somewhat deeper; and there was often a gentle concave bulge in the middle. Plates with very broad, flat rims enjoyed great popularity in the following century.

In discussing English pewter, a distinction is often made between plates and chargers, the latter being normally much wider. They were not used for eating from, but for serving food. The earliest known English plates date from the

beginning of the 16th century and are similar to modern saucers in shape. Seventeenth century plates are characterised by a number of reedings or raised circles running parallel to the rim, which, in turn, is often relatively wide. However, by the beginning of the eighteenth century the design had become simpler, and a single reeding is more common between 1700 and 1750. An interesting charger, with

a single reeded rim and decorated with wriggled work, is illustrated on page 25. Such chargers, here with the owner's initials or coat of arms in a cartouche, often formed part of a dowry or marriage settlement. From about 1730 a plain design with a broad, unreeded rim became popular. Another form that became fashionable was the octagonal or decagonal plate, with a circular centre and straight rims. A fine pair of octagonal plates are illustrated on page 29.

Spoons were another item of tableware frequently made in pewter, and some very early examples have survived. This is partly because of their small, compact shape, but more likely because they were normally beaten when being manufactured in order to stiffen and harden them against rough usage. Archaeologists have dug up spoons from 14th century sites; a well known early type is the 'maidenhead' spoon, so called because the figure forming the knop is said to be the Virgin Mary. The more common 'apostle' spoon, representing one of Christ's disciples on the knop is also found in pewter. Later portrait spoons are sometimes called 'Hanoverians': these properly date from the Georgian period and have a somewhat flatter bowl than earlier types. Examples are known with relief portraits of Queen Anne and Queen Charlotte, the latter probably cast on the occasion of her marriage to George III.

Another common piece of pewterware is the porringer, a shallow square-shouldered bowl used for serving porridge or such like. About six inches across and two or three inches deep, a porringer normally has one or two 'ears' projecting flatly from the rim to act as handles. The whole would be cast in one piece, and a great deal

Drinking vessel in the shape of a Bible. A clear example of the weird creations spawned by a desire for novel drinking forms. The inscription indicates that the 'bible' was a vessel of the Shipbuilders' Guild. Unidentifiable marking, c. 1600. Height: 18 cm.
Paperweight in the shape of a skull, c.1600.

of trouble went into the design and decoration of the ears, which became more sophisticated with the passage of time. It should be also noted that the single ear became fashionable during the latter part of the seventeenth century, a trend that continued until well into the eighteenth. Porringers can sometimes be confused with quaiches, which are found only in Scotland, and though similar in shape served a quite different purpose, as a drinking vessel for toasts. Examples in pewter are very rare.

Kitchen and household pewter

Kitchen pewter includes saucepans, colanders, tubs, various kinds of moulds (for puddings, sweetmeats or ices) and also such items of cutlery as scoops and ladles. It is not easy, however, to draw a dividing line between kitchen pewter and tableware, since many household utensils were used both in the kitchen and at table.

When during times of war pewter was collected or requisitioned for gun-founding, it was the simple pewterware of the home that was the first to be melted down; for this reason few early examples have been preserved. But the basic forms have barely changed over the centuries.

Pans

Food would be carried to the table in large covered pans, shaped like cauldrons; on either side were flat projecting ears (mostly cast in decorative relief), to which was attached a swing handle. Since the dining hall and the kitchen often lay some distance apart, a steady stream of fresh hot food in small pots was kept up throughout the meal. One example of this type of vessel that was common in Germany is the so-called *Hangelpott* ('hanging pot') or *Seeltopf* ('soul

A pair of octagonal English plates. Early eighteenth century, 8 inches across. The straight edged design replaced the round shape at the end of the seventeenth century, and remained popular until the development of porcelain ware 75 years later.

pot'), spherical in shape, with a drawn-in foot or circular base and a flat-domed knobbed lid. These 'hanging pots' were used not only to carry the food out but remained on the tables as serving dishes.

An English solution to this problem was the hot water plate or dish, which had a double bottom that could be filled with hot water to keep the food on top warm. Such plates were also made in pottery.

Pewter saucepans are something of a rarity: the low melting point of the alloy did not make it an ideal material in the first place, and many pans must have perished from being left too near the hob!

A large household would also have a certain amount of medical and sanitary ware, and here again pewter can be found used - with

left Doll's kitchen. Square, mounted on a four-legged frame, painted with a wood finish. Features an open hearth with chimney-seat and a border running around it on which are sixty pieces of kitchen pewter, seven pieces of earthenware, a bronze mortar, and a brass pan. Mid-19th century.

right An English double inkwell and penholder (standish) with two wells and drawers to hold pens, knives and so on.

good classical precedent, for pewter is one of the materials named by the doctor Galen (AD 129 - 199) along with glass, horn and silver as being suitable for medical use. Such ware would include bleeding bowls (often like a barber's basin, with a section scooped out of the rim), bed-warmers, designed to hold hot water rather than the ashes found in their copper counterparts, and pap-boats used for feeding invalids and infants. Babies' feeding bottles in pewter are also known.

An important feature of any household - and a source of interest and variety for the collector - is the candlestick. Candles were the single most reliable form of lighting until late in the nineteenth century, and so candlesticks, candelabra and lanterns offer a vivid picture of social life. Candle holders would vary both according to their purpose, from the simple pan, thumbpiece and socket adequate

for a servant's bedroom to the ornate and multi-branched candel-abrum for the dining room, and according to the owner's pocket and taste. In general the designs on pewter followed the fashions of silverware, save that pewter was very rarely engraved. So the plain forms with reeding on the pillar of the late seventeenth century gives way to the Adam and Corinthian designs of the suceeding century, and in turn are replaced by the bulbous balusters of the Victorian era.

We cannot leave the subject of household pewter without some mention of two sorts of pewter with a great deal of appeal to collectors, namely salt and pepper pots (the word cruets is here reserved for ecclesiastical objects), and inkstands. Salt was for a long time an expensive commodity, and so early salts do not often show a generous space to hold the precious article! In the seventeenth century the bobbin or capstan shape was

Two Deckels-choppen of the Shipbuilders, and a filter which was filled with spices and immersed in the hot drink. *Left*, 'fine metal' mark: Martin Brandt, Hamburg, master 1734. *Right*, 'fine metal' mark: Claus Gohrt, master 1797. Heights: 31 cm and 27 cm.

popular, and this developed into a proper cup shape in the eighteenth. Later designs, as with pepper pots, became more fanciful, the forms of birds and animals being adapted for the purpose. Inkstands also developed in decoration from the formal square type, often with drawers in the stand, as seen on page 31, to the florid creations of the Victorian era. In one respect the collector of Victorian pewter, which can fascinate for its very variety, should beware: a great number of Victorian pieces were made not in true pewter but in Britannia metal. This alloy has a different composition from pewter, is considerably stronger and can be cut by lathe or pressed from

left An early French flagon with spout: marked Leclerc, Lille.
below left A group of three Channel Islands measures. The central one is the Jersey type, in which the plain body rises directly from the feet. Those on the left and right are Guernsey measures, with reeding around the body and an indentation to separate the feet. The capacities of such measures, made until the early nineteenth century were peculiar to the Channel Islands. The design is also unique to the Islands.

below Another pewter shape found only in the United Kingdom is the Scottish measure, called a tappit-ten measure. These three flagons are good examples of the shape, with flat or decorated lids. The word tappit-hen correctly refers to the quantity (three pints) but is now used to describe the shape.

sheets. The resulting products have a different finish and the metal is often thinner. It lent itself, therefore, to the rather heavy and finicky decoration beloved of some Victorians, and being easier to mass-produce, led to a decline in traditional cast pewter working.

European styles in pewter

If one starts to look for particular *national* differences in pewterwork, one has to admit at once that, with the exception of a few special types, the forms of everyday pewter, determined as they are by their function, are more or less

Three screw-top bottles. Round bottle with double band of punched ornament and ring-handle. Unmarked. End of 18th century.

Square bottle with flap-ears on either side and a tall cover. The top part of the screw-lid is itself unscrewable; this suggests that it may have been a child's bottle. Unmarked. End of 18th century.

Hexagonal bottle, engraved floral and foliage ornament. Inscribed on the body L. St. Two marks-Urach, 18th century, Johann Georg Buhler the Elder, 1744-1777.

Swiss Sugerli (water jug). The vessel has a spout cast as a relief mask and an iron hook. 'Surgerli' and 'Brunnkesseli' are names given to the special form of feeding-pot with hinged lid that was prevalent in the 17th and 18th centuries. It was hung by the hook and used as a swivel pot. The Sugerli is assumed to have been used to feed children because, as with babies' bottles, the mouthpiece has a thickened end which often appears badly worn. A fine rosette on the base but no discernible marks. Northeast or Central Switzerland. Mid-18th century.

Glockenkanne. Bell-shaped flagon with moulded 'running dog' decoration and bayonet-joint lid. The thin angular spout is fitted with a little hinged cover which features

an escutcheon containing the initials I.K. and the date 1745. Mark: Lindau, and lion issuant. Maker: Johann Baptist Ernst. Mid-18th century. Height: 31 cm.

Screw-top bottle with carrying clip. Octagonal body, lathe-turned. Screw-lid. The fixed angular clip is of iron. c.1700. Mark on the lid: Nuremberg, c.1700. Height: 28 cm.

standard everywhere. Furthermore, everyday pewter is not easy to categorize on the basis of a precise chronology of styles, since a pewterer would often adhere to a traditional form long after styles had changed; it sometimes took more than a century for the adjustment to be made. It was common practice as early as the start of the nineteenth not only to use old pewterware for decoration but also to have replicas made of well-known traditional forms. Needless to say this did not always result in the happiest blend of styles.

Great Britain

In general, as we have seen,
English pewter followed forms
common elsewhere, save in that the
alloy used in pewtermaking was
considerably finer than some other
European versions, and consequently
needed less decoration. However,
there are certain pewter designs
specific to the British Isles,
particularly the forms used for
wine, beer and spirit measures.
The baluster measure, in which the
body swells out from the foot and
then tapers in to the distinctive flat
lid, is found only in Great Britain.
The general shape of the baluster
body can be seen in the right hand
illustration on page 23, though the
piece shown has a domed lid. The
lid would often carry a maker's
mark or inscription identifying the
innkeeper who owned it. The
Weights and Measures Inspectors
would be responsible for stamping
the capacity on the piece, often on

the rim, a process known as
sealing. The type of seal used is a
guide to dating ware: the most
desirable pieces date from prior to
the introduction of Imperial measures
in 1826, and carry the crowned W.R.
of William III, who introduced an Ale
and Wine Standard in 1688. Another
method of dating, as with tankards, is
according to the thumbpiece used on
the lid, such as ball and wedge, bud
or double volute. With the
introduction of Imperial measures
the baluster types became less
frequent, and unlidded, bulbous
measures popular.
The baluster form was found
particularly in England, for in
Scotland, Ireland and the Channel
Islands there were also local forms
of measure, of which the Scottish
'tappit-hen' measures are the best
known. The general shape of such
measures can be seen from the
illustration on page 33. The title
given them is perhaps a corruption
of the Old French *topynett* or quart:

a similar derivation from Old French is found in the name 'chopin' for a 1½ pint measure. Thus a tappit-hen is correctly a measure of three pints, but the term is now used to describe the shape of measures of different quantities. After the introduction of Imperial measures the thistle shape (with a knop half way up and flared top) was, appropriately, used as a spirit measure: many, however, were confiscated and destroyed on the grounds that they did not deliver the full quantities.

Channel Islands measures are illustrated on page 32: the form with reeded decoration was peculiar to Guernsey, and the quantities contained in the different measures followed the system native to the Islands until the introduction of Imperial measure. Not surprisingly the general design of Channel Islands pewter is as much reminiscent of French shapes as British.

Irish baluster measures are distinctive because they rarely have handles: such measures usually are for half-pint, gill, half-gill and quarter-noggin sizes, though the smallest often has straight sides in place of the usual baluster curves. After the change to Imperial, measures in the 'haystack' or 'harvester' shape were made, with conical bodies resembling the traditional rounded Irish haystack.

National variants

France

There is evidence of a major pewter industry in France from the 15th century. In addition to display vessels cast in relief there existed an extensive range of household pewter: plates, pots and other items of tableware in forms that are smooth and simple, yet well proportioned. A small jug – the *pichet* – was the most common pouring vessel. The earliest examples date from the 15th century and retained their basic baluster form up until the second half of the 18th century. The pichet has a slightly protruding lip, a tall stepped-pyramidal base on top of which a conical lower section supports the belly of the vessel. The type found in Normandy has a low, barely suggested base with a cylindrical body and solid drawn-in neck; while the Lyons variant takes the form of a tapered body with cylindrical base and mouth. Lidless *pichets* are also found, as are jugs that are a mixture in form of *pichet* and vase – a type that has been much imitated.

The simple, unadorned *aiguiere*, a big-bellied water jug, developed in the course of the mid-16th century into the magnificent 'arabesque' flagon. The *cimaise*, found in the Champagne region, is a ewer with a tall moulded base and a short

Plate. Twisted loop decoration with cross fluting. On the plate a view of Zurich, inscribed Die obere Stadt zu Zurich ('The upper town in Zurich'). Mark: Bernese arms, 1729.

'Cardinal's hat'. This is the imaginative name given to broad-rimmed plates and dishes which resemble a cardinal's hat from the underside. The broad rim, reinforced with a strengthening edge underneath, is usually flat and engraved with nothing more than a crowned monogram or coat of arms indicating ownership. In this case the owner's initials are H.M.H.

Two Hangelpotte ('hanging pots') and a 'ring' jug. The 'hanging pot' or Seeltopf ('soul pot') is a distinctive North German type, a spherical body with drawn-in foot capped by a flat-domed lid and knob. A hinged clip was attached to ears at each side (usually with relief-cast decoration). These covered pots were used mainly for conveying food.
The 'ring' jug (also known as 'prismatic' jug) derives its name from the ring-handle attached to the lid.
All three vessels are unmarked. 17th – 18th century. Pots approx. 20 cm high, jug 34 cm high.

Two hot-water bottles. In the winters of earlier centuries bed-warmers were indispensable items for unheated bedrooms, journeys, and going to church. They are shaped like a loaf of bread (round and oval) and are fitted with a screw-cap. Left: the hinged ring on the bottle bears foliage relief. Two marks on the screw-cap: Master Johann David Hochel the Elder, Backnang; Master David Hochel the Younger, 1749. Diameter: 23 cm. Right; hot-water bottle with twisted ring. Unmarked. 18th century.

Chamber-pot. This is the most common form, i.e. spherical with a flat collar. Mark: Johannes Reinol, Ulm, 1821-1891. Height: 12 cm.

Wash-tub, potbellied with broad carrying clip. Illegible marking. c.1600. Height: 36 cm.

Jug. This was probably an oil-jug or a spirit-flask. The thumbpiece is shell-shaped. Mark: Vintrin Montpellier. Early 18th century. Height: approx. 20 cm.

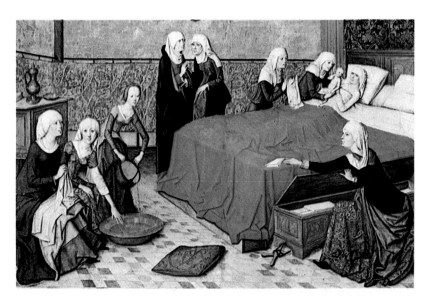

stem; the basic baluster design of the body occurs in various forms and is surmounted by an expanded, hemispherical mouth with a corresponding domed cover. The scalloped swing handle had its pivot joints near the top edge. The *cimaise* also has a fixed handle.

The broad-rimmed dishes known as 'cardinal's hats' from their shape in profile, which are found in Germany, were also used in France as game dishes.

Switzerland

Swiss pewter was always especially rich in peculiar variants of the standard forms. Indeed, in 1610 a decree was issued in Basel aimed at designs of no practical use: 'In

'The Birth of the Virgin Mary', oak, 85 × 109 cm. Master of the Life of the Virgin Mary, 1460 – 1480. Notice the footed jug and other items of household pewter. 15th century.

view of the many masterpieces (i.e. pieces produced by craftsmen qualifying for the rank of master-pewterer) that are unusable and hence unsaleable, more practicable arrangements are in future to be made so that such pieces may be of use and financial interest to the layman'.

The fact of the different cantons having such sharply defined customs underlies this predilection for special forms. Some of the most popular types may be described here. The *Stegkanne* derives its name from the crosspiece (*Steg*)

Pewter candlesticks are recorded as early as medieval times. Their size varies according to function. Secular candlesticks were often adorned with inscriptions, dedications, and bequests. The pewter candlesticks produced in the 18th century copied forms taken from other materials.

From left to right: candlestand, dated 1727; candlestick of the Sailmakers' company, dated 1798, mark: Gottlieb Kare, Hamburg, master 1798, died 1828; candlestick on square base, inscribed: Der Ewerfuhrer vom alten Kran, dated 1806; small candlestick with baluster-stem, dated 1728; candlestick of the Sailmakers' company, unmarked. Heights: 18-28 cm.

Three coffee-pots. The shape of their lids led them to be known as Turkenkannen ('Turkish pots'). The handles are all of wood. The middle pot bears a mark: Johann Hinrich Plan III, master 1777. The pot on the left is dated 1796, the pot on the right 1830. Heights: 26-28 cm.

Four oil-lamps. Instead of a candle these oil-lamps (known affectionately as Ölfunzeln) have a small tray attached to the shaft in which oil (rape or cobra oil) is burning using a wick. In the middle is a night-light, a Funzel with a glass container for the oil. The frame was normally marked with an hour-scale, which would indicate the time during the night according to the oil-level. In former times it was customary to sleep by a night-light. Unmarked.

which forms the connecting piece between the shaft and the tall-bellied body – although usually not on a perfect plane. It was also used widely by guilds in Germany.

The *Glockenkanne* ('bell-shaped pot') with its round tub-like form, its typical screw lid, and its vertical ring-handle, is still produced today. The most popular of all these forms was probably the Valais wine pitcher. Related to the French *cimaise*, it has a compressed spherical belly mounted on a narrow beaded foot. The top third of the wide neck broadens out to form a bowl with a slight point for the spout. The lid is flat and usually heart-shaped, with an 'acorn' knob and a flat handle.

The *Kelchkanne* ('goblet pot') is a variant with a circular stand instead of a footring, and a body that is a gently widening cone, rather than a rounded sphere. A third variant is found only in Valais: the body has the form of a truncated cone and is surmounted by an expanded mouth with a flat lid.

Most of the special forms of Swiss pewter occur only in the context of the so-called *Schutzengaben*, prizes awarded at shooting contests, whereas the ordinary pewter tableware is similar to that produced elsewhere.

Overleaf: Garland of guild shields. Guild shields are emblems cut from sheet pewter and often adorned with engraved figures and vessels. They were hung out either in the guild hostels as a guide to travelling journeymen or in the taverns to indicate a guild's regular drinking table. The surviving examples date from the 18th and 19th centuries, although it is reasonable to assume that guild shields were made from pewter long before that. In recent times old guild emblems have been re-cast using rubber or plastic moulds. The shields shown here are all of the 18th and 19th centuries.

Pewterer with flat-bottle; strapmaker with bundle of straps. Pen-and-ink drawing with colour wash, c.1580.

Austria

It is almost impossible to make an adequate stylistic distinction between the pewter of multi-national Austria and that of its neighbours; in general, the standard household items manufactured in Austria since the Middle Ages adhere closely to the range of forms that prevailed in neighbouring countries.

Netherlands

The wealth and prosperity which the Dutch had achieved through the enormous expansion of trade in the 16th and 17th centuries are reflected in imposing collections of household and kitchen pewter. In addition to the Hanseatic flagon, dating from the early 14th century,

there developed other distinctive pot types which bore close stylistic links with north German forms: the Bossian pot, already described, is one example; another is the 'Rembrandt pot', squat and pear-shaped in appearance, with a broad neck and a low, cylindrical base, partly drawn in. The origin of the name remains a mystery, since Rembrandt never depicted a vessel of this kind in his paintings. The 'Jan Steen pot', on the other hand, does indeed owe its name to the famous artist, who was fond of including such pots in his still-life and genre paintings. The distinguishing feature of this pot is its long and angular lidded spout, rising steeply from the belly and enabling wine to be poured with style in a high arc.

The Dutch pewterers retained most of the time-honoured forms until well into the 19th century.

Sweden

Here also the Hanseatic and central European designs are found in the pewterware of daily life, and especially in enormous pots, plates and dishes.

North America

Pewter was used in North America mainly to produce simple household pieces, in accordance with the

Detail of finial on the lid of a Willkomm. The Willkomm was a ceremonial drinking vessel used as a loving cup by the guilds for special occasions. The normal form was that of a goblet or tankard. The example shown here was used by the Hamburg Bakers' company. Marked 1643, stamp worn off. Inscription on the flag: Sie laben. Height: 64 cm.

Willkomm of the Hatters and Feltmakers. Several dedicatory shields are hung around the cup, which bears the date 1821. Mark: Hermann Daniel Meyer, Lubeck. Height: 55 cm.

Two Willkommen. Left: Willkomm of the Shipbuilders. Dated 1736, marking illegible. Height: 67 cm. Right: see 47.

needs and wishes of the settlers. Their forms were determined by the traditions prevailing in the immigrant pewterers' country of origin; the most common are English. Before the war for American independence, the British government imposed duty on exports of raw tin but not of finished ware, so that it may be presumed that much early American ware was reworked from older finished pieces. There are few wholly American designs, but one curiosity that deserves mention is the lamp designed for burning whale oil: these were mainly manufactured in Boston.

The Pewter Guilds

The guilds developed all over northern Europe simultaneously with the development of town living from the 12th century onwards. In continental Europe it was in the interest of the towns to encourage craftsmen of all kinds and the steady employment that a system of guilds could guarantee, since the availability of craftsmen not only strengthened the economy in peace time but provided a reservoir of skills in time of war. In the British Isles, the guilds provided safeguards against competition both within and from without the country. Because much early British pewter was, it would seem, destroyed in the Civil War, and, as has been mentioned, the

Pewterers' Hall burnt down in the Great Fire of London, most of the examples of Guild pewter shown here are from the Continent.

The first Royal Charter was granted to the 'Craft' (or 'Mystery') of Pewterers in 1473, although it is clear from earlier records that the guild was already established at that date, and had already specified in their Ordinances the terms of apprecticeship and the

Tobacco-bowl of the Hatters' and Feltmakers' company. The bowl is shaped like a hat. Dated 1824. Touch of Martin Johann Hinrich Dahm, born in Lubeck, died in Hamburg 1824. Height: 13.5 cm.

The shape of the hat is clearly seen when the bowl is turned over.

basic requirements as to standards. This was well established in London, and the Charter granted by Edward IV extended the authority of the guild over the whole of England, giving them the right to search for and confiscate goods of inferior quality or poor workmanship. The extension of this power over the whole kingdom is evidence of the importance of the pewter trade. Provincial cities were not slow to follow London's example: the Ordinances of the York Guild were published in 1419, 1456 saw those of Bristol published, and the Hammerman of Edinburgh became incorporated forty years later. That these ordinances codified long standing practice is shown by a reference in the document recording the establishment of the Bristol guild to the hammering of vessels 'that ought to be beat after the rule of the Craft of old time used'.

By controlling, through power of search and seizure, the manufacture and so to an extent the market for pewter, the Company could regulate recruitment, as it were, and thereby ensure a reasonable standard of collective protection for its members. The affairs of the Company were controlled by its Court, consisting of the Master, two Wardens and the other Past Masters. They set the term of apprenticeship (normally seven years, but sometimes extended to

Vexierkrug of the Wheat-bakers. Dated 1787. Touch of Johann Jurgen Christoph Sommer, Hamburg.

ten) which had to be served with a Liveryman of the Company. On completion of the apprenticeship the apprentice would be presented to the Court by his master, and show a test piece of his own making. He now became a Freeman or Yeoman of the Company, and was entitled to 'open shop and strike his touch', with the permission of the Court. Often a young man who had finished his apprenticeship would not have the capital to start in business for himself at once, and would work as a journeyman for another until able to do so (for this reason there are discrepancies in dating between a person receiving his freedom and striking his touch). Once established in business in his own right, the

Ashtray of the Ladlesmiths' company.
Dated 1841. Illegible marks.
Diameter: 26 cm.

Two Willkommen. Left; Willkomm of
the Undertakers. Inscribed on the
body: Wie bluhende Rose ('Like a
blossoming rose'). Silver dedicatory
shield. Dated 1830, Hamburg.
Illegible marks. Height: 53 cm.
Right; Willkomm of the Millers'
company, with pendant richly
embroidered with pretzels and other
emblems of the trade. Dated 1811.
Touch of Bernhard Johann Fahren-
kruger, Hamburg, master 1798.
Height: 65 cm.

Guild flagon and guild cup. Left:
flagon of the File-cutters' company.
Guild flagons are pouring vessels
of similar proportions to the
'dragging pot'. The type shown
here, with a spherical belly mounted
on a high base, originated in the
second half of the 16th century.

Two guild flagons. Left: flagon of
the Blacksmiths' company, with
engraved names. Dated 1750.
Touch of Johann Mathias
Timmerman the Elder, Hamburg,
1718-1784. Height: 33.5 cm.
Right: flagon of the Blacksmiths'
company, with engraved names.
Dated 1768. Touch of Johann
Mathias Timmermann the Younger,
Hamburg, master 1751. Height
34 cm.

pewterer could hope to be elected
a Liveryman, with the right to take
apprentices himself and with the
hope of election to the office of
Steward, Warden or Master. This
process ensured a gradual pro-
gression: an order of the mid-
sixteenth century forbade an
apprentice to be made free until he
reached the age of twenty-four.
'Striking a touch' meant entering
the personal punch or mark on the

touchplates at the Pewterers' Hall. This touch, like the maker's mark on silver, should be made on every piece he manufactured and sold. It was a guarantee to the customer that the piece came from a proper craftsman, and proof of origin if any dispute arose. Some touches carried the full name, some just initials; often they would show a rebus or pun on the pewterer's name: it is not difficult to guess the surname of TB who showed a bell between the two letters. Mr Adams, whose mark showed his name above a man and a woman in a garden, displaying more originality. Some touches are quite anonymous: one such shows a rampant unicorn with the hopeful inscription 'let trade flourish!' The original touch-plates at Pewterers' Hall were destroyed in the fire in 1666, though the practice of striking touches dates back to the start of the 16th century at least. New plates were purchased when the Hall was rebuilt, and, it seems likely, pewterers who were already free were invited to re-strike their touches. The practice continued until the decay of the Pewterers' Company as a trade guild at the start of the 19th century. A full list of the marks, with reproductions of the touchplates, can be found in Howard Cottrerell's *Old Pewter, its Makers and Marks*. The only mark a piece of pewter should carry is the touchmark, though several additional marks are found, for example the rose and crown mark, believed to have been for export wares and a mark of quality, as was the X mark. Some pewter pieces carry 4 small marks resembling hallmarks, a practice that led to considerable complaints from the Goldsmiths Company! Unlike silver, pewter did not legally need to be marked, and the absence of marks does not mean that a piece is either of poor quality or counterfeit. Apart from the regulation of membership of the profession, the Pewterers' Company also laid down rules for the quality of material used: the earliest ordinances (those of 1348 already referred to) set standards for the different alloys that by and large remained constant. For sadware (or flatware, such items as dishes, chargers and plates) an alloy called 'fine metal'

had to be used consisting of 26 pounds of copper to every hundredweight of tin. For hollow ware (rounded items such as flagons, tankards and cups) 'lay metal' could be used, for which 26 pounds of lead to every hundredweight of tin was required. This softer and weaker alloy was permitted, presumably, because the shape of

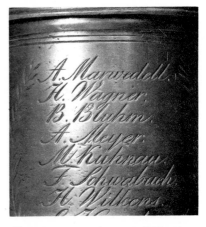

Names engraved on a guild beaker using a burin. Mid-18th cent.

such pieces would give them additional strength and support. But the fragility of lay metal was evidenced by the introduction of 'tryfill', an alloy made up of equal quantities of new fine metal and recast lay metal.

These standards were the ones used by the Company's searchers when assaying pewter in dispute. The method used was to compare a sample of fixed size of the disputed metal with a piece of tin of the same size: the difference in weight would show the proportion of lead or copper added. The records of the Court of the Company show frequent occasions when pewterers were fined for failing to mark their wares, and, less frequently, had wares confiscated because they were below standard as to metal content. For

Dish, mounted on three ball-feet with a movable ring-handle. Engraved inscription and 'wriggled work' floral motifs. Dated 1793. North German. Diameter: 25 cm.

example, Humphrey Westwood and Thomas Cowes were brought before the Court in July 1595/6 for making eardishes and beakers 'of false metal, 4 grains worse than lay'. The wares were forfeit, and the miscreants ordered to make good the losses incurred by those pewterers who had bought the pieces. Furthermore, Westwood was asked to bring in his touch for

replacement by a double ff (perhaps meaning 'fined for falsehood') and also provide sureties against his future conduct. The control of marks was important to the Company, and when in the later part of the 18th century the control could no longer be enforced and so was dropped, the decline of the pewter trade as a craft guild trade began also. However, the Worshipful Company of Pewterers is still a Livery Company of the City of London, sixteenth in the order of civic precedence. The Company continues to take an interest in the craft, both by supporting technical education and by forming a collection of historically important pewterware.

Guilds in Europe

In the towns of northern Europe, guilds developed on much the same lines as in England, save that they took further the principle of collective protection both of consumer and producer. Guild membership would be enforced as a prerequisite to starting in business by the municipality, with a like obligation on the citizenry to support local businesses. The guilds in some cases also controlled the supply of raw materials, to ensure fair and even competition. In times of economic prosperity, and so long as the authority of the guilds lasted, this system worked

Tavern shield of the Potters'
company of St. Georg und Stadt-
deich. Marked Hamburg 1834.
Height: 34 cm.

Offering-box of the Bell-founders.
The money collected in such a box
was intended for the sick and the
orphans of a guild, and came in
usually as 'fines' levied for breaches
of guild regulations. Marked 1683.
No stamp.

Tobacco-dish of the burial fund.
The tobacco-dish illustrated here is
decorated with monograms and the
inscription: Der wahre Glaube eines
kanaanischen Weibes ('The true
faith of a woman of Canaan').
Marked 1767, AB 712.

well. But the guilds built up around
themselves elaborate codes of
honour and secrecy, and became
institutions frozen in past custom
rather than responding to current
events. As a result the European
guilds did not last as long as their
English counterparts. Being based
on rather smaller communities,
however, the guilds, particularly
those of Germany, would be more
convival, and it is not surprising
that much of the guild pewterware
that has survived was used for
drinking and eating. One such
piece is the cup known as a
Wilkomm (or *viderecome* in France).
This was a large, two handled cup,

Candelabrum of the Shipbuilders. Marked 1794. Maker: Gottlieb L. Kraeftl, Altona, master 1756. Height: 70 cm.

Candelabrum of the Shipbuilders. Engraved monograms adorn this Neoclassical candelabrum. Beginning of 19th century. Gottlieb Kare, Hamburg, master 1798, died 1828.

often with a separate cover, which would pass around as a loving cup at guild occasions, with much ritual and ceremonial. The name literally means 'welcome': not surprisingly the cup would also be brought out from its place of honour on such an occasion as the freeing of an apprentice from his indentures or the promotion of a journeyman to higher rank. Incidentally, the European journeyman was often just that; someone who had completed his apprenticeship and was travelling around and working in other towns to gain experience before returning home to set himself up in business. The

dragging pot or *Schliefkanne* was another guild object. Used on the occasion of an apprentice being 'freed', the pot had to be filled by the new freedman or journeyman with beer for the company. This required a flagon far too heavy to lift! The dragging pots had faceted sides, often decorated with religious or secular pictures. Other, more common objects, such as tankards, flagons and tobacco boxes, are found today in German museums: such pieces may often carry an inscription or insignia to show that they were for guild use.

The Pewter Maker's Art

Das Zinn mach ich im Feuer
  fliessend,
Tu danach in die Model giessen,
Kanndl, Flaschen, gross und auch
  klein,
Daraus zu trinken Bier und Wein.
(I make pewter liquid on a
  flame,
Then pour into the mould,
To fashion pots and bottles,
  large and small,
From which to drink beer and
  wine.)
Der Kanndlgiesser (The Pewterer),
lines by Hans Sachs, 1568.
Its bright and silvery shine and
excellent properties have assured
the base metal tin of a constant
and varied use since ancient times.
We cannot say at what point in
history mankind first recognised tin
to be a useful metal and what he
then did with it, but we know from
archaeological finds that tin was
valued at a very early stage in
human history.
The metal that has the chemical
symbol SN (Latin *stannum*) is an
element belonging to group IVa of
the periodic table. It seldom occurs
naturally in its pure form, but is
usually found as the ore cassiterite
(known also as tinstone). Cassiterite
is tin dioxide (SnO_2) and forms the
base material for the mining and
extraction of the metal. The
primary deposits are found as
mining tin, which is tinstone
ocurring in hard lodes or veins and
crushed on the spot (as with coal
or iron ore). Rare scattered
deposits are found in granite, mica,
hornblende, or argillite.
Alluvial deposits are secondary
sources; the metal found in such
deposits is known as *stream tin* and
is formed by the gravity separation
of cassiterite from decayed tin-
bearing rock debris; the ore is
washed away and deposited in
streams where the water flow is
slack.
Both types of deposit may be
found in strata several metres
thick.

Tin extraction

The extraction of mining tin is a
lengthy process. In order to extract
tin from cassiterite, the ore is first
fed into rolling mills, where it is
crushed, sorted, and washed by
ball-grinders and steam hammers.
Subsequently roasting removes
impurities such as sulphur and
arsenic, and a further heating in
either a shaft furnace or a

Pewterer's workshop. Mid-18th cent.

View of a French pewterer's workshop. After an engraving taken from Salmon, *Art du Potier d'Etain,* Paris 1788.

Casserole. This kitchen piece is not only of superb design but also provides an excellent example of a successful combination of pewter and brass. The brass elements (feet, handle) have been soldered on. Unmarked, c.1820. Height: 18 cm.

Underside of the base of a mug, showing mark where beaten out. After the pewter had been chilled in the mould (whether 'lost' clay or metal mould), the solidified object had to be beaten out. The pin holding it in the mould is clearly visible in this example.

Vegetable dish. Straight-sided dish with flat well and movable curved handles. Gadrooned ornament on the outer surface. North German. Unmarked. Mid-18 cent. Diameter: 24.5 cm.

reverberatory furnace releases the remaining impurities such as iron. After smelting, the raw tin, which has a low melting point (231.9°C), is channelled over a sloping surface which retains the more refractory iron. This process, known as liquidation, is followed by a further refining before the purity required for commercial use is reached (98.60 – 99.98% tin). This method of production is still the most common one today and has changed little since ancient times. Stream tin, exposed as a result of natural weathering, is simply washed out of the debris; this process, known as 'soaping', was

used particularly in East Asia. In spite of primitive working conditions the Chinese applied skill and persistence to achieve excellent results.

A distinction must be made between *white* tin, which crystallizes in a tetragonal structure, and *grey* tin, a semi-metal with diamond-type cubic structure which will eventually disintegrate into a powder. Tin is tougher than lead and can be rolled out into very thin foil or tinfoil. Natural oxidization of tin takes place at a relatively high temperature, and it is resistant to weak acids.

Tin and other metals

Tin occurs in many combinations, of which the most important is without question the copper-base alloy which has given its name to a whole historical period: bronze. This compound with its reddish gold lustre, is so tough that it was used in making effective weapons as well as jewellery and utensils. As early as the third millennium BC, bronze – and therefore tin – was known to the Persians, Babylonians, Sumerians and Egyptians, and also to the civilisations of India and China. In the course of the following millennium the Phoenicians, the most important trading and sea-faring nation of antiquity,opened up the trade routes of the ancient world; at first this meant only the Mediterranean region, but later the Phoenicians extended their routes to reach England, Scandinavia, Russia, and the Germanic tribes.

Mining areas

At about this time the Cornish tin-mines were opened; they remained an important source of tin until well into this century. The principal tin-producing areas today, Bolivia, Malaysia, Indonesia, were also known in ancient times. In the 12th century AD a new supplier appeared alongside the old tin-producing areas when the tin-mines of the Erzgebirge mountains on the border between Saxony and Bohemia were opened. Their heyday came in the 16th and 17th centuries.

Marseilles, Cologne, and Bruges were all important centres of trading and reshipping at this period; so also, at a later date, were Nuremberg and Augsburg. The Thirty Years' War had a severely damaging effect on production levels of tin, and the subsequent recovery in the late 17th and early 18th centuries was a slow one. Then, in the first half of the 19th century, cheap crude tin from rich overseas deposits began to flood the European market, producing a crisis which proved decisive: the trade based on the Erzgebirge, once so flourishing, now faded away and with it a cultural phenomenon that had long been of such significance: pewterware.

Tin alloys

Beside bronze there were many other combinations in which tin was used, the pure metal being far too soft for casting on its own. When the crude tin arrived, in ingots or balls, it was combined with other metals; it was the addition of copper or brass, or even on occasions a little bismuth, that gave good, clear, pure pewter. The addition of lead, however,

produced the commonest form of pewter, known as 'lay metal' or 'test pewter' (German *Probezinn*). Lead increases the workability of the cast metal and its subsequent hardness, but excessive quantities can have a toxic effect, especially when, for example, a vessel made from this alloy comes into contact with certain acids. For this reason there were regulations, dating right back to medieval times, which laid down the proportions of tin and lead that were permissable.

From the second half of the 19th century it became common practice to add antimony to tin, giving rise to an alloy known as 'Britannia metal'. Nickel, zinc and bismuth were also alloyed to tin in this period, with the primary aim of giving the metal a silver-like appearance.

The working of pewter

Tin has to be melted down and cast, since it does not possess the density or workability of silver or copper and will not endure being forged or hammered out in its natural state.

Melting and casting

The cast metal is liquefied in a

Views of the old pewterer's workshop in the Weygang Museum, Ohringen.

Types of pewter decoration

above Rosette soldered onto the base of a tankard to fill the hole left by the lathe spindle.

below Etched decoration on the footrim of a tankard, applied by cutting onto the surface with acid.

facing page, above Punchmarks, made by striking the surface with a metal tool carrying the negative impression of the mark.

below left Engraved decoration or wriggled work, made by rocking a broad bladed tool or burin across the surface of the metal.

below, right Decoration cast in relief (in the mould) on the handle of a flagon.

crucible, then scooped out with a ladle and poured into the prepared mould. Moulds were the pewterer's treasure, and many examples survive from the past. What they were made from depended on the financial circumstances of the particular pewterer: thus we find moulds of sandstone, or plaster, brass (from 1550), and even of iron and pewter itself (from the 18th century).

In the Middle Ages castings were made from 'lost' moulds. The molten metal was poured into a

cavity formed between a clay core a clay case which corresponded to the shape of the desired vessel. Once the metal had solidified the mould was smashed and then it was simply a matter of turning off any irregularities on a lathe and of polishing. The lost wax process, or *cire perdue* casting, was reserved for the more artistic products because of its high cost.

The choice of temperature at the casting stage is critical for the ensuing processes. If the temperature is too low, then the finished

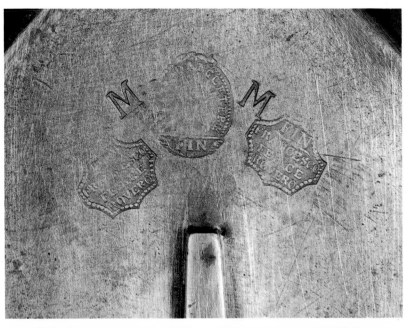

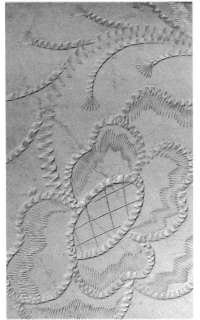

article will be dull and porous, a condition known in German as *kalkbruchig* ('lime-short'). If the heat is too great, then the metal changes colour and becomes *rotbruchig* ('red-short'). The mould has to be firmly clamped together by means of grooves, plugs and pins, to prevent the molten metal escaping. If the metal does not fill all areas of the cavity, the casting will have pores or holes and will be useless.

The beauty of a perfectly cast, unadorned piece of pewter is indisputable. Nevertheless, pewterers in all ages have sought to decorate bare surfaces in the hope of increasing their value as ornaments.

Decoration

Relief decoration is a type of ornament created during the casting process. There are many different ways of producing it, the oldest of which is the working of the mould with a burin or graving-tool; the motifs thus engraved appear in relief on the finished product. This method found its most widespread use in 16th century France and in Nuremberg in the late 16th and early 17th centuries.

Between 1560 and 1590 the Nuremberg pewterers developed the technique of etching the negative motif on the mould, so

Elements of a mould for casting a wine jug. Figs. 1-7, for the neck; figs. 8-12, for the base; figs. 13-16, for the handle; figs. 18-30, for the hinge and the lid; fig. 17, how a handle is 'burned' onto the body of the vessel; figs. 32-36, the individual cast pieces for the wine jug; figs. 37-40, the mould for casting the neck of a jug.

that the impression on the casting appears to be raised and sharply outlined, but is nevertheless relatively flat. The relief worked on two levels only since the acid had a corrosive, not a moulding effect. The similarity of this process to woodcuts led to it being known as the 'woodcut' style.

In Saxony relief work was produced in a much simpler and more convenient fashion. Ready-made relief plaques in lead, bronze or pewter were purchased and joined to one another in rows; casts were then taken in plaster, pewter or lead, from which a positive was subsequently struck.

However much the techniques for producing relief pewter work may have been developed, the use of this type of decoration remained restricted to ornamental wares such as were displayed on pieces of furniture or hung on walls (whence the term 'display pewter', German *Edelzinn*).

Engraving is a decorative technique that was frequently applied to pewter surfaces, since the

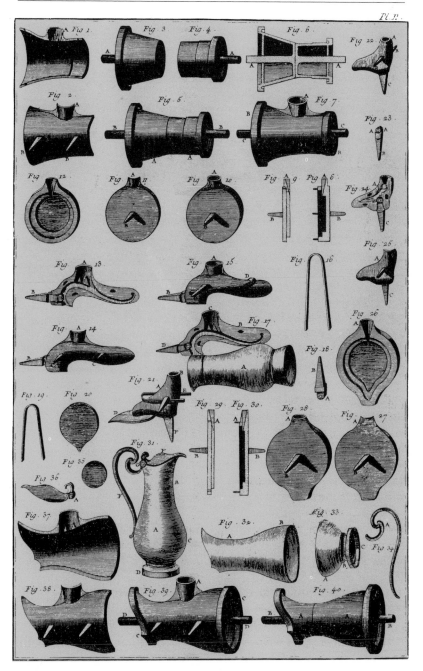

soft nature of the metal affords
plenty of scope for ornamental
work of this kind.

Where the lines of a pattern are
continuous, as in pen-and-ink
drawing, we refer to it as engraving
or cutting. In the case of point-
work, also known as stippling or
pointillé decoration, the lines are
composed of small dots punched in
the metal.

The most common form of
engraving is 'wriggling' or 'joggling',
where the linework is produced by
a rocking motion of the chisel or
scraper to give a zigzag effect.
Plant motifs feature particularly in

Rorken or Weinkroos of the
Pewterers. Marked 1660. Maker:
Jurgen Lutkens T. Hamburg, 1634-
1660, master 1660.
Tankard of the Ropemakers'
company. Marked 1699. Maker:
Peter Jost von Stade, Hamburg,
master 1662, died 1704.

this type of decoration, since they
help to underline its pictorial
qualities. English pewter does not
by and large, go in for elaborate
decoration. There are two possible
reasons for this, one general, one
rather more specific. The general
reason is that English taste in the
17th and 18th centuries at least

A coat of arms made of sheet brass. It has been set into the lid, and engraving has then been used to blend it optically with the background.

Detail from a double door, part of the house of an important official in Hamburg, c.1720. Oak with horn-beam and box-wood marquetry. Engraved pewter inlay. The surface ornament has been carved out and filled with pewter, a technique applied especially to furniture.

did not run to extremes of fancy and ornament. The silverware of the period shows an equal restraint. Also, pewter being regarded as a definite second to silver at that time, no-one was probably very interested in paying high prices for fine workmanship. That said, it must be admitted that good English pewter can show an excellent sense of controlled design. The more specific reason is that the Pewterers' Company preferred to keep all working of the metal to their own members. There is a record of a Freeman being fined for using an outside engraver

to work on a finished piece instead of a member of the Company. Such an attitude may well not have encouraged pewterers to look for decorative skills in the workshop. Engraved work was normally executed only at the request of the client; in other words, the pewterer did not keep stocks of engraved pewter, but worked to order. The designs used in such work range from elaborate figurative and landscape compositions to simple geometric patterns and monograms.

Chasing or 'tooling' was a favourite technique for decorating pewter during the Renaissance. It involved the use of an iron punch, the end of which bore a small negative impression. The punch is struck hard into the pewter surface, producing a pattern composed of little ornamental

feature - e.g. acanthus-leaves, pearl-clusters.

A type of decoration rarely practised on account of its costliness was that of **etching**. The pewter surface was covered with wax and the background that was to appear sunken was scraped out, leaving the design itself still under wax. Acid was then allowed to react on the surface, producing a low relief.

Intaglio, or incised relief carving, was another rarely applied technique, where the background was removed directly to leave a patterned surface.

Hammered pewter work is also rather rare since the metal, unlike copper, brass and silver, will not endure stretching and thinning in individual areas. The only decoration of this kind is found in rows of small motifs that have been beaten out with wooden mallets.

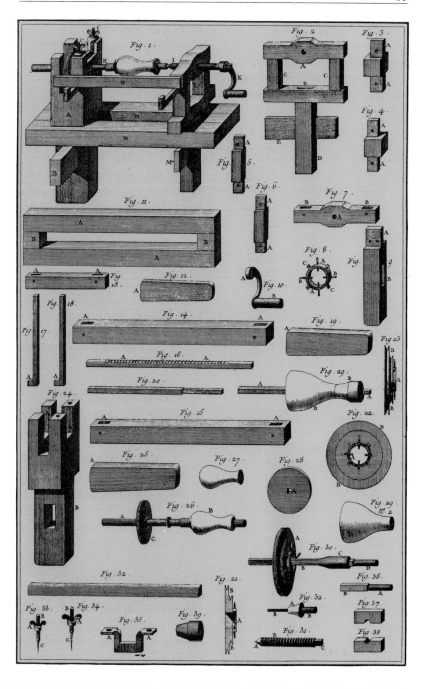

Fig. 1. Fig. 2. Fig. 3. Fig. 4. Fig. 5. Fig. 6. Fig. 7. Fig. 8. Fig. 9. Fig. 10. Fig. 11. Fig. 12. Fig. 13. Fig. 14. Fig. 15. Fig. 16. Fig. 17. Fig. 18. Fig. 19. Fig. 20. Fig. 21. Fig. 22. Fig. 23. Fig. 24. Fig. 25. Fig. 26. Fig. 27. Fig. 28. Fig. 29. nº 2. Fig. 30. Fig. 31. Fig. 32. Fig. 33. Fig. 34. Fig. 35. Fig. 36. Fig. 37. Fig. 38. Fig. 39.

This technique is not to be confused with *repoussé* work, a type of embossing that became frequent in the 18th century, where the drums of tankards and flagons were hamered out in ribs and grooves.

Beating pewter is one means of refining the pewter surface. Beating is a simple forging process, where the hammer-blows are applied in regular circles, thus forming a concentric pattern.

Inlay. The combination of pewter with other materials is particularly attractive. In the second half of the 16th century brass was much used as an inlay in pewterware, especially in northern Germany. Particular parts of the vessel (the spout, handle, grip, lid, foot, ring, hoop) might be made completely of brass, affording a contrast between its golden colour and the dull silvery lustre of the pewter. Alternatively, ornaments of brass or brass plate might be 'appliqued' to the surface of a finished vessel. Brass was also used as an inlay in surfaces that had been specially punched out.
Pewter inlay work is to be seen on so-called 'Lichtenhain tankards': decorative motifs, cut from sheet pewter and usually bearing engraved details have been set into the outer surface of these wooden stave-pots. The mount is also of pewter. The use of pewter as an inlay in doors and furniture was confined largely to aristocratic circles. Pewter and tortoiseshell inlay in furniture was made famous by André-Charles Boulle in Paris.

In the age of display pewter **gilding** and silvering were both processes applied to pewterware, although in the lean period following the Thirty Years' War they were restricted in the main to church plate. Melchior Koch (16th century) was the master of pewter gilding.

Painted pewterware is known to have been quite common in France from the 17th century. It is by no means easy, however, to apply a coat of paint that will last; moreover, this form of decoration does not seem to suit the material. In the early 19th century two-tone and even colour transparent lacquers were applied to everyday objects. Strong colours were the most popular: yellow, green, red, black often with decoration in gold or other contrasting colours.

If a piece of pewter was made up of several parts, these would have been soft-soldered in most cases, or occasionally stuck together or welded. Besides pewter itself, any binary material containing tin, lead, bismuth or cadmium was used for the solder. A fluxing agent was usually added to facilitate wetting;

Stoneware tankard with gilded pewter mounts. The painted terracotta depicts a hunting party. Since pewterware loses its character when gilded this technique is extremely rare. Prussia. Dated 1673.

any traces of it that remained after the soldering were washed off. The operation was normally carried out with a soldering iron and a gas flame.

Another method of joining or affixing parts to finished forms was that of 'burning on'. The mould was altered in the appropriate place, sealed with clay and then filled. A piece of moistened linen was placed over the area and held firmly in position by clay to prevent any of the molten pewter escaping. Often one finds the pattern of the linen preserved in the cast metal.

Pewter lids were fitted on jugs and tankards of glass and faience as well as on pewter vessels themselves, a process known in Germany as *Aufgiessen* ('casting on'). First the lid was cast onto the hinge by filling a small loam mould formed between the two elements, then another mould was built up around the mug-handle and hinge,

'Travelling pewterers'. Caricatures after 18th century engravings. Taken from Tardy, *L'Étain francais*, Paris 1959.

and filled, the hollow space being produced by using a strip of leather removed before casting.

Special care must be taken in the working of pewter after casting. First the casting rivets are cut away, then any fins and other rough spots are filed down. The piece is next fixed on a lathe by means of a suitable wooden chuck, and the dull skin of the casting is turned off by hand. Eventually, after agate has been used to polish up the surface at the same time as it is kept moist by soapy water, the warm shine of the pewter will appear. The surface of the finished, soldered piece is then burnished with little, fast-rotating pads (of leather or cloth) to give it a silver-like finish. Brass-wire brushes are used to give pewter its characteristic soft and silky lustre.

After polishing, a piece of pewter may still be coloured, in which case it is dipped in a dye-bath to produce tints ranging from silver through grey to black. This process is often used in an attempt to give an antique look to a piece of pewter. Tinting can also be achieved by brushing the surface after it has been coloured.

Thus the completed pewter article needs a considerable number of processes carried out by different artists and craftsmen (founders, turners, polishers) between its design and its completion.

Display Pewter

The sixteenth century marked the turning-point in the development of the pewterer's craft in Europe, for now, in addition to being the source of an extensive industry manufacturing household wares, pewter entered the realm of fine art. To use Demiani's words, 'by "display pewter" we understand those pewter objects which were fashioned to a degree of artistic refinement beyond the requirements of function, being, indeed, mainly designed as showpieces.'

The golden age of pewter had begun. The terrors of the Thirty Years' War had been left behind and the supremacy of the guilds during the Renaissance brought wealth and power to the towns, which in turn led to improved living conditions and to more refined customs.

Display pewter owes its development to a passion for collecting which seized both aristocratic and bourgeois circles in the latter half of the sixteenth century. Not only was there a delight in the richness and beauty of natural forms and materials, but a new interest was awakened in art itself, indeed in the art of all ages and nations. The skill and mastery of the craftsman at work excited as much admiration as did his artistic achievements. Displays of technical virtuosity, even if they resulted in shapes which seem strange by today's standards, were received as enthusiastically as were those strange natural phenomena that were collected as curios with such avid delight – especially when they came from distant lands. The riches of the Kunst Kammer – a room or cabinet for the display of curiosities, relics and treasures – are evidence of a lively period in the history of culture, and create an impressive picture of its beliefs and ideas about art.

The transition from the late Gothic to the early Renaissance is reflected in the development of pewter. The severe ornamentation of the Gothic style gave way to a greater plasticity in cast figures. Throughout Europe the sixteenth century was a time when artists and craftsmen turned their attentions to producing secular objects, whether for everyday use or as pure ornament. And the greatest master in this respect was Benvenuto Cellini. It was through his connection with the Florentine Mannerists that the influence of his art extended to France.

The style of Italian mannerism, as

Temperantia Ewer. The surface is divided horizontally into three bands and the neck, on each of which figures, ornaments, and cartouches have been cast in fine relief. On the lowest band, on the shoulder, and on the neck: grotesques, masks, and strapwork. On the middle bank: three oval cartouches with the allegories of the theological virtues and their Latin names Fides (faith), Caritas (charity), and Spes (hope); arabesque surrounds. The high handle is adorned with masks similarly cast in relief.

The Temperantia Salver or Dish belonged to the Temperantia Ewer. Until the 18th century meals were mostly eaten with the fingers; between the courses or afterwards the guests would wash their hands in water poured by the servants from jugs into shallow basins. This simple operation developed into an elaborate ceremony using the precious salvers and ewers, which were displayed for all to see on the large sideboards. The Temperantia ewer and salver belong to the same tradition as the rosewater basins

made by the court goldsmiths. Maker: Francois Briot, born in Damblain c.1550, last mentioned 1616. Master in Montbeliard from 1580. Ewer and dish can be dated 1585/90. The Temperantia Dish carries relief decoration on the base and rim. The boss in the centre shows Temperantia, or Temperance, surrounded by representions of the four elements Terra (earth), Ignis (fire), Aer (air), and Aqua (water), set against a lush landscape background. The rim contains eight oval medallions featuring Minerva and the seven liberal arts, interspersed with four masks. On the underside a portrait medallion of Francois Briot, inscribed: Franciscus Briot sculpebat. Diameter: 45.5 cm.

Detail of Ewer. Central cartouche. Allegorical figure of Pax (Peace).

A Temperantia dish. Only thirty of these treasured works of relief pewter still survived in 1920. The virtue Temperance is seen clearly in this illustration, appearing as a female figure seated on a goat and holding a wine bowl in one hand, and the wine jug in the other. The stylistic influences can be traced back to the work of the Strasbourg ornamental engraver Etienne Delaune and to the murals in the Chateau of Fontainebleau, executed from 1532 by the Italian painter and decorator Francesco Primaticcio together with G.B. Rosso and others.

Example of the so-called Fama salver. Fama or Fame is shown allegorically as an angel bearing a cornucopia, surrounded by rich foliage ornament. The relatively shallow relief decoration has been cast in an etched mould. Classical figures and scholars amidst arabesques. Around the edge birds of paradise. On the booge the initials AP and an angel with cornucopia. Maker: Albrecht Preissensin, master 1563, died 1598, Nuremberg. c.1560. Diameter: 28.5 cm.

'Pyramus and Thisbe' dish. Relief decoration cast in the mould. In the base a representation of Pyramus and Thisbe and the four elements (water, fire, air earth). Around the edge the story of the Fall, interspersed with masks. In the spaces arabesques and palmettes. Inscribed: SRNR. Unidentified mark. Nuremberg work, after 1600. Diameter: 46 cm.

Lappenteller. A relief plate in the manner of the heraldic plate, but with cut-out round arches surrounding the coats of arms. (Instead of being completely circular, the rim thus has 'lobes', German Lappen.) The form was created in St. Gallen as a 'Ruttli Oath' plate by the mould-engraver Zacharias Taschler. St. Gallen, c.1700. Diameter: 14 cm.

it was practised in France with its almost excessive profusion of form and thematic ingenuity, found its most magnificent expression in a courtly total work of art: the Chateau of Fontainebleau. François I was the royal patron who engaged the services of a group of Italian architects, painters, and sculptors who formed the nucleus of the first School of Fontainebleau. Although designing few buildings himself, the architect and painter Serlio who

was summoned to France c.1540, exercised a lasting influence through his theoretical writings on architecture; while in the plastic arts it was the 'elongated' forms of Primaticcio that served as models.

Francois Briot and French relief pewter

The work of Francois Briot, the most celebrated pewterer of the mid-sixteenth century, is based on the stylistic principles of the School of Fontainebleau. Briot came from Montbeliard in Lorraine and was active until 1585 as coin-engraver to the Duke of Wurttemberg. The riches in the Duke's large treasury doubtless served as an inspiration to Briot when he was designing his magnificent pewterware. The real secret of Briot's art, however, lay in mould making and in casting technique. Whereas in the past it had been the accepted practice to engrave or solder on decoration after casting, the design was now worked into the mould itself, requiring as much ability on the part of the mould-cutter as from the pewterer himself, who put all his professional skills to the test in producing perfect castings of these large objects with their many curves and edges.

The models for the decoration applied to this kind of pewter were those ornamental engravings which were so common in the 16th century and did much to popularize the decorative forms of the Italian Renaissance throughout Europe. The distinguishing feature of this style was the revival of classical Roman forms. The wall-paintings in ancient Roman houses, with their carefully combined compositions of plants, candelabra, figures, and various hybrid forms, were emulated and developed in strange and wonderful ways by artists of the Renaissance. The Mannerist artist-craftsmen evolved from this a system for the shaping and patterning of vessel surfaces which led to highly inventive compositions. Although the essential features of this system remained unaltered over a long period, there was a fairly rapid change in its *formal* nature. Thus in the latter half of the sixteenth century we find applique work that appears to have been fashioned from interlacing metal bands, a type of ornament known as strapwork. By the turn of the century the strap-ends appear in relief, as if rolled up; indeed, the general style at this time comes to be dominated by the increasingly popular motif of the volute. In the first period of Baroque ornament in the early seventeenth century the so-called *Knorpelstil* ('cartilage style') turns the scroll into a more gentle, plastic device, often with an anthropomorphic character.

A predilection for the grotesque was a feature of all these designs, as was the fact that they retained a connection with the human form; indeed, foliage and the human face were sometimes combined to produce strange masks. These 'foliage faces' had already appeared in the ornament engravings of the early sixteenth century; a century later they had come to constitute an important feature of the *Knorpelstil*. The latter half of the

above Pair of candlesticks. Typical Baroque form of baluster-stem set on tripod. The tripod is decorated with tendrils and strapwork cast in relief. First half of 18th century. Unmarked, probably Augsburg. Height: 23 cm.

right In the foreground, Branntweinschale ('brandy bowl'), a typical North German drinking vessel with flat side handles (usually with pierced ornament). 18th century. *Behind*: two salts with relief decoration (one engraved, the other etched). 18th century. Both unmarked. Heights 26 cm and 23 cm.

far right, top Bowl. High rim with deep spiral fluting. Angel-mark and maker's mark: Johann Georg Neeff, Frankfurt am Main, master 1770, died 1802.
Helmkanne ('helmet jug'). Frankfurt am Main, 18th century. Unmarked. Test piece, showing unpolished casting bur.

right, centre Covered tureen.
Oval base, body and cover
decorated with rocaille relief. Knob
in the shape of a Baroque vase.
'Fine metal' mark and maker's mark:
E.F. Karlsbad, 1774. On the
underside of the base the inscription:
Kampfet kluger, Bohme, 1781
('Fight more wisely, Bohemains,
1781').

right, below Coffee-pot. The pot
is fashioned in the 'silver manner', a
term referring to pewterware that
has been given a surface of
scalloped ribs like the high-quality
silver work of the Rococo period.
'Fine metal' mark: Bohemia, *c*.1700.

Chocolate-pot. 'Silver-type' pewter.
Three angel 'fine-metal' marks: EAG,
mid 18th cent. Maker: Johann
Adam Gwinner, Ohringen, 1731-
1782. Height: 9.5 cm.
Coffee-pot with knob-handle. 'Silver-
type' pewter. 'Fine metal' mark:
maker Johann Georg Klingling,
master 1726, died 1749. (The
Klinglings were a family of pewterers
resident in Frankfurt am Main who
remained active for more than 200
years. In the 18th century the
Klingling masters were so successful with their 'silver-type' pewter that
their business was more like a
factory, their products sold to bulk
purchasers and wholesalers.)

seventeenth century witnessed a further elaboration of foliage ornament in lavish acanthus designs, whose leaves were shaped into scrolls to give a strong impression of three dimensions. The subjects that were treated in this style were allegorical; to the common medieval allegories relating to theology and Christian morality there had now been added a range of subjects derived from classical mythology.

The Temperantia Ewer and Dish

Among the masterpieces created by Briot are the so-called Temperantia Ewer and the Temperantia Dish. The ewer, also known as the Briot Vase, belongs to that type of French pouring vessel derived from classical models: a beaker form resting on a base, with a drawn-in neck. The vessel is decorated with the allegorical figures of Pax (Peace), Temperantia (Temperance) and Mars (God of War), together with ornamental motifs.
The boss in the centre of the dish also features the figure of Temperantia, seated on a pedestal with a drinking bowl in one hand and jug in the other. She is framed by a wide frieze containing allegorical figures of the four elements set in oval cartouches,

Milk jug, with wave patterns running round the surface. The jug stands on four Baroque cartridge-feet. Marked: 1/249, James Dickson and Sons, Sheffield, 2624. 18th cent. Height: 15 cm. Tea-pot. Potbellied body mounted on shell-feet. Running guilloche engraving. Same marking as the milk jug, but with the number 214. Height: 15 cm (approx.).

between which appear winged caryatids. The rim of the dish has eight oval medallions in the midst of a wealth of grotesquerie; these show Miverva as the guilding force of the seven liberal arts - grammar, arithmetic, geometry, music, astronomy, dialectic, and rhetoric. The elegant, elongated figures demonstrate clearly the influence of the Fontainebleau school. According to Demiani, Briot chose this particular motif because he believed that the forces of Nature herself looked favourably on the practising of art.
The ewer and dish were intended for washing hands at the Royal table. They are the only works by

Tea-caddy, in the shape of a cupboard, and with a double lid. Chinoiserie reliefs on the surfaces, surrounds of ornate strapwork. 'Fine metal' mark with the inscription: IE. Maker: Johann David Grober, Augsburg 1750-1767. Height: 16.5 cm.

Spoon board. Trefoil with animal hanger. Thirteen pewter spoons, with the inscription: AR, 1829. The board is unmarked, but the spoons carry marks. 1829. Height: 33.5 cm, width: 28.5 cm.

Briot to bear his signature – the letters F.B. cast into the metal. The dish, moreover, is also marked with a medallion on the reverse side, showing a bust of the master together with his signature. The characteristic pewter stamps are missing.

The Nuremberg relief pewterers

As a result of standing trial for debt Briot was obliged to part with his moulds, which were subsequently put to use by many other pewterers. This is the reason why there are so many copies of the Temperantia dish with marks of various other makers and towns. The most impressive pieces worked in the manner of Briot's reliefs were those produced in Nuremberg by the masters Nikolaus Horchhaimer, Jakob Koch II, and Kaspar Enderlein, a native of Basel. Koch developed a technique which gave his pewter a startling appearance, 'as if the objects had been gilded, and with gold of such high quality that they preserved this look even after long and regular use'.

The pewterer and mould-cutter Kaspar Enderlein became a master and a citizen of Nuremberg in 1586. He owed his popularity to his skill in engraving relief decoration on casting moulds. His moulds were made for the use of other workshops, since they bear not only his initials cut into the mould but the marks of different master pewterers. The effects of

Overleaf: Two ink-wells. Right, ink-well of the Sailmakers, dated 1794. Touch of Carl Georg Buttner, Altona, master 1781. Left: ink-well of a fraternity, dated 1752. Illegible touch. Heights: 8 cm.

Coffee-pot. Engraved surface decoration showing foliage-work frieze. Tall raised spout with animal mask. The angel mark on the base is indistinct. End of 18th cent. Height: 21.5 cm.
Sugar-bowl. Unusually well-executed 'joggled' work showing vine-leaf decoration. Mark: angel mark. Maker: Johann Georg Gunzler II, Rothenburg ob der Tauber, 1833/54/74. Height: 17.5 cm.
Covered bowl. Twisted webbing in imitation of silver. 'Fine metal' mark dated 1710 (or 1719); 'fine metal' mark with initials WE. Maker not identified. Height: 12 cm.

Enderlein's work were felt in this way until well into the 18th century. The Nuremberg city register of deaths reveals that forty-four pewterers died there during the second half of the 16th century, and fifty-six between 1600 and 1660, but only fourteen during the first half of the 16th century. It can thus be seen that c.1600 Nuremberg was not only the home of famous masters like Enderlein, Horchhaimer and Koch II, but the undisputed metropolis of German pewter. As a comparison, according to Cotterell's researches, about 150 pewterers were registered by the London Company at the middle of the seventeenth century: a finding based on the re-striking of touches after the Great Fire.

The Nuremberg Pewterers' guild saw this trend towards concentration with some misgivings, and endeavoured by tightening up the existing rules and taxes to maintain the high artistic and qualitative standards of Nuremberg pewter work. For example, No.11 of the pewterers' ordinance of 1576 contains in clause 2 the following ordinance, which soon became obligatory throughout Germany and established the superior quality of German pewter: all pewterers were forbidden, under oath, to treat beaten (stamped) or English pewter differently from pure pewter unalloyed with lead; objects of beaten pewter must be stamped with an eagle and a crown, those made and finished in the English way must bear an eagle, a crown and a rose.

The bold sweeping forms of High Baroque and the delicate ornamentation of Rococo, with its playful asymmetry and gently curving ribs, could be executed easily enough not only in silver but also in the pewterer's mould. Consequently, pewter came to be known as 'poor man's silver'. We know in fact of many cases where clients approached a pewterer with the designs of a particular silver 'garnish', wishing to have them copied in pewter as faithfully as possible. As early as 1629, at the wedding of the Habsburg King Ferdinand, pewterware is said to have been made that was based on silverwork from Prague and Vienna. One device which the pewterers clearly imitated was the Baroque flowers of Nuremberg and Augsburg silver, found in relatively shallow relief on plates but more deeply on other objects, such as screw-top bottles. Pewter had already been worked in Europe in the manner or silver in the sixteenth and seventeenth centuries; indeed the whole notion of relief pewter had been conceived in close imitation of embossed silver work.

Augsburg, Frankfurt, Karlsbad

In the Baroque and Rococo periods the focal point of the pewter business shifted from Nuremberg to Augsburg, the great centre of silversmiths in Germany. Besides the Augsburg master pewterer Sebald Reprecht there were also in Frankfurt and in Karlsbad a number of skilled artists who created splendid pewter work in the Baroque manner. The pewterer's art was given another huge stimulus by the magnificent table silver of the age; its lively Rococo forms were copied in pewter, above all in France and Germany.

above Sugar-bowl (the cover is missing). The circular holder is pewter relief work, featuring a frieze of standing sphinxes. The three lion herms which carry the holder are themselves mounted on a wooden tripod. Unmarked. 1810-1815. Sugar-bowl. The oval holder is decorated with swags of fruit and wave-pattern friezes in finely-wrought pewter relief. Unmarked. c.1800. The inserted bowl of cobalt glass dates from the beginning of the 19th century. Height: 14 cm.

facing page Picture-frame. The ornament of festoons and amphorae makes this a typical Empire piece. The portrait is of Christian A. Weygang, born 1747, who in 1777 founded the Weygang pewter works in Goppingen. Unmarked. c.1800.

Pewter in the age of Neoclassicism and the early nineteenth century

With the discovery of porcelain by J.F. Bottger and E.W. von Tschirnhausen in Dresden in 1708 pewter was faced with serious competition. The ordinary bourgeois tended to use the cheaper materials faience and earthenware, while at the courts pewter was replaced gradually in the course of the eighteenth century by the new material porcelain, until by the end of that century it had disappeared almost completely from use. We have already seen to what extent the influence of the Pewterers' Company in London fell off during the eighteenth century: in England also pottery and porcelain manufacture, as well as imports from China, must have reduced the market for pewter. Only in rural households and in the context of guild life did pewter retain its significance. Furthermore, bad, shoddily executed copies of older models were now being made and damaging the reputations of the real craftsmen working in pewter. Declining

demand fatally undermined the pewterer's creative instincts, with the result that many master craftsmen were forced to suit their products to prevailing tastes simply to keep themselves alive.

With its striving after a restrained simplicity in form and design, Neo-classicism, the movement which began around 1800, could never do justice to the warm, full-blooded material that is our subject. Severe courses of garlands, acanthus leaves, and rosettes now constituted the decoration on urns and amphorae, and on flagons and tankards.

A common feature of the Empire period is the bronze mounts with motifs derived from classical antiquity; these are found fastened particularly to little items of ornamental tableware such as salts, sugar-bowls and candlesticks. The pierced salts are given coloured-glass insets.

Among the larger articles in daily use made in this period, and corresponding in their forms to contemporary silverwork, are coffee-pots in the characteristic Louis XVI style; tureens with flat handles that are either auriform or else raised and angular; and elaborate centrepieces. With their extensive surface areas, pewter wall fountains, first produced in the Baroque period, provide good examples of the thin and sparing ornamental

'Eternal flame' lamp. Three crowned bird's heads as handles. Unmarked. Beginning of 19th cent. The ampulla is 18.5 cm long.

style of Neo-classicism.

Around 1800, some fifty years later than in other areas of the applied arts, a few pieces in the *chinoiserie* style were produced in pewter. The fashion for things Chinese had first appeared in the European deco-rative arts at the beginning of the eighteenth century and had been encouraged by the growing quantities of imported Chinese porcelain. The distinctive lightness and lability of Chinese forms were copied in cast relief work, especially on tea-caddies.

Between the Napoleonic Wars and the 1848 Revolution in Germany there unfolded the Biedermeier Age, whose principal characteristic was a harmonious relationship between man and his domestic environment. The word Biedermeier can be roughly translated as 'honest but narrow-minded'; it was arrived at by combining 'Biedermann' and 'Bummelmeier', two characters created by the writer Viktor von Scheffel to represent different aspects of philistinism. The period to which it gives its name was for a long time dismissed somewhat mockingly as 'fussy', although it was in fact the last stylistic epoch with any real sense of homogeneity. The greatest effect of the Biedermeier was to place domestic culture on a more human and personalized level. A new and simple world of forms was created on the firm base of bourgeois realism. The notion of the modest, natural idyll now replaced that of high-flown emotionalism. The utterly unacademic art of interior design attached the greatest importance not only to good, solidly-made furniture, but also to those 'accessories' (tableware, etc.) that enhanced the quality of life. As a result pewter came to enjoy a renewed esteem, even if few actual innovations in the pewterer's craft were made in this materially deprived age, where the moulds of previous styles, such as Empire and Louis XVI continued to be used.

Pewterware was often enamelled and painted in bright colours in order to assert itself against the many pieces of coloured glass made in this period and against the increasingly widespread use of porcelain. In the country especially, domestic pewter continued to be manufactured in the traditional manner.

Historicism – fantasy-pieces and copies

A sense of tradition also led to that blending of styles, commencing in the mid-nineteenth century, which art history describes as Historicism. Only shortly after the classicizing trends, artistic currents were felt that were signalling a return to the art of the Middle Ages. Unlike Neo-classicism, historicism is to be understood as the first *national* retrospective style; in the course of the century it was followed by other manifestations of national reminiscence.

The medieval household supplied as few models for the everyday articles of the 19th century as did classical times. We find certain Gothic motifs used as stock elements: pointed arches, pilasters, foliage work, gargoyles, all combining to form ornamental friezes and decorative schemes that

Flagon. The polygonal body is richly engraved with figures of saints (full-lengh, half-length, and busts) beneath tracery canopies. In the centre the Virgin Mary and the seven Virtues. On the lid a representation of the Last Supper. The flagon has a spigot and a twisted handle. Unmarked. Second half of 19th cent. Height: 60 cm. (According to the records of the Weygang Museum this is a copy taken from an original in August Weygang's workshop.)
Stangenpokal. Lavishly engraved with foliage-work, coats of arms, and strapwork decoration. The final is an eagle with outspread wings. A clear example of the over-elaborate use of ornamental devices that was characteristic of the pewterware of historicism. Unmarked. Second half of 19th cent. Height: 59 cm.

were applied to the furniture and utensils of the period. The idea was to create pieces in the Gothic style as they would have appeared had there in fact been a need in the Middle Ages for the clock-bracket or the floor-vase. Icono-graphical and literary allusions from the medieval world were also used, from the Crusaders and noble ladies of the early romances down to the gnarled portraits of craftsmen in the late Gothic churches of Germany.

Once more a lively demand for pewterware prevailed in the age of the Altdeutsch ('old German') style. The suppliers of these wares, however, were not so much pewterers with their small work-shops as manufacturers using mass-production techniques.

Lavishly decorated pewter mugs and tankards are evidence of the misguided impulses that drove people not only to revive old styles but also to reconstruct the relevant forms in a much 'purer' and more stylistically 'faithful' manner; in other words, to make the Gothic 'even more Gothic', to make the Romanesque 'perfectly Romanesque'. In Britain, revivals succeeded each other thick and fast, leading to the crescendo of the Great Exhibition of 1851, in the Crystal Palace in Hyde Park, where the Victorian taste for narrative decoration combined with their zeal for mechanical ingenuity. Pewter did

Covered goblet. The goblet shows pseudo-Baroque elements in both design and decoration, combined to form a rich ornamental composition. The foot and the cup are fashioned in elaborate curves, and around the vessel there runs a banderole bearing the inscription: A von L 1683. The date refers not so much to the year of manufacture as to the stylistic affiliations of the ornament. (floral garlands, cartouches, etc.). The lid is crowned by a thistle. Angel 'fine metal' mark. Maker: Kayser, Offenbach, c.1890. The initials F.D. in the mark. Height: 45 cm.

however, an interest has begun to be taken in the problems and stylistic phases of historicism, and in producing a more critical evaluation that had been possible in the past, when people simply turned up their noses at this period in the history of art.

not play a large part in this development, for it was still a traditional craft technique, unvisited by the benefits of the Industrial Revolution. However, the Victorian period saw the heyday of Brittania metal instead of pewter (much as electro-plate was regarded as more modern than silver). So the heavy and bulbous decoration of the era is frequently found on Britannia metal teapots, vases and pots. Traditional pewterware continued to be made in the old forms. Whether or not one chooses to collect the pewter work of this period is a matter of personal taste and attitude. In recent times,

In contrast to the archaizing creations of the time we also find pewter pieces which have been produced as direct *copies* of historical originals. The favourite models were those with relief decoration, since it was simply a question of taking casts from them; these replicas can be identified by the relief work, which is less sharply drawn than on the original on account of the additional casting process.

Besides the copies of relief pewter produced at this time, we also find plates with imitations of antique engraving; these have usually been given a false year of manufacture.

By the end of the century copies were also being made of tureens, mugs, dishes, candlesticks, bowls, porringers, and all kinds of household ware. The client could choose between a 'high-polish finish' and 'delivery in attractive original colouring'; for purposes of decoration the latter option enjoyed the greater popularity.

Josef Lichtinger of Munich must be mentioned in particular for it was to his orders that artists such as Stuck, Gabriel von Seidel, and Seder worked, producing the desired models in a style known as the 'Makart style'. Flagons and drinking beakers featured especially.

Lichtinger, together with the outstanding engraver Roder, created objects that are significant for their high standard of execution, even if they are rather strange in design.

Although products of the Neo-Gothic and the Neo-Renaissance movements were by far the most common in this period, there was also a revival of Baroque and Rococo forms of decoration. Articles of the Neo-Baroque and Neo-Rococo were produced in the manner of silverware; they were made mostly from alloys which looked like a precious metal. Britannia metal is the best-known alloy of this type; it contains

antimony, is shinier than pewter, and does not require excessive care to preserve its appearance; it does not, however, attain the brilliant lustre of silver.

Just as Britannia metal looks like a hybrid creation, so too the objects that were fashioned from it have no style of their own, nor do they correspond to the style of either pewter or silver. Orivit was the name given to another alloy produced at this time, of tin and silver.

The stimulus that had been given to pewter manufacture in the 19th century was of an economic rather than an artistic nature. Only in the late nineties did a movement emerge whose declared aim was to free the applied arts from the fetters of historicism and to create something fundamentally new and *sui generis* as a way out of the crisis of artistic design. Art Nouveau, 'Modern Art', and Jugendstil are the names given to this endeavour to breathe new life into stale forms.

Bowl, *c.*1905. The long flowing hair surrounding the delicate girl's face (with roses over her brow) forms contours that glide all over the surface. The design is from the *atelier* of Engelbert Kayser, the execution by J.P. Kayser & Son, Krefeld-Bockum. Marked with an oval company stamp and the number 4495. Height: 6 cm; diameter: 15 cm.

One of a pair of Fledermaus candelabra. The so-called 'bat' candelabra were designed by Engelbert Kayser; they provide an excellent example of the fusion of form and theme which he strove to attain. The candelabrum is composed of three hunchbacked bats, whose outspread wings form the branches. Executed by J.P. Kayser & Son, Krefeld-Bockum. Marked (on the underside of the base): oval company stamp and the number 4506. Height: 30.5 cm.

Detail of *left* showing clearly the harmony of outline between artifact and natural form.

Art Nouveau Pewter

On 15 February 1901 there appeared in Munich the first edition of the *Deutsche Zinngiesser* (German Pewterer), a trade journal for pewterers, engravers, zinc-workers, brass-founders, and other related professions. It included the following article, under the heading 'Invitation to subscribe':

'The venerable trade of the pewterer, whose coat of arms bears the bell and cannon as well as the pewter flagon and goblet, has in recent times been steered by modern trends along paths which have brought it high artisitic esteem. The saying 'not to go forward is to go backward' should apply to anyone involved in a trade or business, and it is therefore important that all craftsmen, all traders, all manufacturers should keep themselves well informed of all the new developments in their particular area. To meet this need vigorously and effectively is, in the first instance, the task of the specialist press: the high reputation it enjoys in professional circles is a measure of its achievements. With the sincere resolve to help the trade in every possible way we bring before the public our 'journal for German pewterers'; it would be our greatest reward if before long

we were numbered among the *essential* specialist publications'.

'Not to go forward is to go backward' was the guiding principle of a major new programme which manifested itself at this time all over the world in the applied arts. Everywhere the spirit was the same, the portents were the same; only the names were different. In France and Belgium this all-embracing movement was called Art Nouveau; in England and America 'Modern style' and 'Arts and Crafts'; in Germany *Jugendstil*; in Holland *Nieuwe kunst*; in Italy *Stile floreale*; and in Austria *Sezessionsstil*. The names may be different, but the meaning is the same: innovation, the incitement to new modes of expression, growing out of a fundamental restructuring, material, spiritual, and social, which was taking place at the turn of the century in each country.

Jugendstil

This German style (which means literally 'Youth style') marks a period in the history of art which has its beginnings around 1880 and has become the subject of lively interest in recent years. This interest has many facets: it does

not restrict itself simply to the realm of art, but embraces the spirit of a whole era, the *fin de siecle* or 'turn of the century'. People look back nostalgically to a world of grandeur, to the society of the Grunderzeit (the period following the establishment of the first German Empire in 1871), but tend to forget the atmosphere of almost revolutionary upheaval that pervaded this same period. The external picture we construct for ourselves is contradictory, therefore, and for many people rests in the realm of purely emotional experience, in a desire to feel part of a past generation. From this it can be seen how broad a field Jugendstil encompasses; its resonances are still felt, even today, if only because it encourages wholly subjective ideas and expectations, most of which have some degree at least of validity.

Rarely has one name been used to describe a style which has so many and different modes of expression. On the one hand there are the luxury products, on the other there is the artistic creed of an age wishing to rebuild the unity of 'art and life'. Indeed, it is a curious injustice that many of the solecisms committed towards the end of the nineteenth century, against which the Jugendstil fought so boldly to release itself and future generations, have in fact been attributed to this very style; plush and palm fronds are all too often thought of as stylistic devices of the Jugendstil.

A factor common to all the artists of this period was the search for a new art-form which would be free

facing page Coffee and tea-service (five pieces: tray, coffee-pot, tea-pot, cream-jug, sugar-bowl), c1900. The severe, straight-sided forms of the vessels and the simple wave-scroll decoration illustrate clearly the search by one group of Jugendstil artists for unconventional designs coupled with objectivity and functionality. Design and execution by the Orivit pewter works, Cologne-Ehrenfeld, Ferdinand Hubert Schmitz. Marked: Orivit and the number 2784. Heights: 11-25 cm.

Detail of the sugar-bowl from another service. Marked Orovit and numbered 2963.

of historicism and academicism. They were no longer satisfied with the eclecticism of previous decades. Standards had been set in literature, in the humanities, in the new technologies, that were no longer matched by the visual arts.

The 1902 Dusseldorf Industrial and Trade Exhibition

The art and trade of pewter were also affected by this atmosphere of upheaval. This emerges clearly from an article which appeared in the *Deutscher Zinngiesserzeitung* on 1 June 1902, reporting on the Dusselforf Industrial and Trade Exhibition.

'Seldom, if ever, can the pewter industry have been as well represented at an exhibition as at this year's Dusseldorf Industrial and Trade Exhibition...

Group 3 gives us a clear picture of the metal industries in the major industrial centres of Germany, amongst which the pewter and Britannia metal industries are, as we have already mentioned, very well represented.....if we consider this group first, then we must begin with the special display provided by the firm of J.B. Kayser and Son from Krefeld-Bockum. Anyone with a specialist knowledge of *Kayserzinn* (the trade name given to the pewter alloy produced by the firm; see below) will be justifiably amazed at what he sees and will have to concede that this world-class firm really has achieved something extraordinary. The modelling and engraving of these works of modern art are brilliantly executed; the

facing top left Two-handled vase, *c.*1905. The continuous guilloche ornamentation is typical of the simple and stylized Nordic variant of Jugendstil. Design and execution by Urania-Zinn, Maestricht, Holland. Marked: Urania.

facing bottom left Full-length mirror, *c.*1900. The basic plant design is broken up by strict, rigid lines decorated with miniature ornament. Executed by Urania,

facing top right Candelabrum, *c.*1905. The designs of the Urania pewter works in Holland were modelled to a large degree on Belgian forms of Art Nouveau. The influence of Victor Horta and Henry van de Velde is clearly discernible here, where the natural form is broken up into a hatchwork of intertwining lines. Unknown designer, executed by Urania, Maestricht, Holland.

facing centre Detail of a triple-branched candelabrum, showing socket and dripping pan.

facing bottom right Cocoa-cup and saucer, *c.*1900. German, probably Darmstadt. The Darmstadt circle favoured more austere forms in its pewterware. Probably executed by the Hueck pewter works, Ludenscheid.

Page 99 top left Jam-jar and plate, c.1900. This design proves that other German pewter manufacturers besides Kayser were also capable of turning out works of real quality and originality. Design and execution by the Orivit pewter works, Cologne-Ehrenfeld, Ferdinand Hubert Schmitz. Marked: Orivit and the number 2079. Height: 17 cm.

Page 99 top right Two-handled fruit bowl. Shape of a trefoil A tree in blossom covers the inner surface of the trefoil in delicate relief. Design and execution by the Orivit pewter works, Cologne-Ehrenfeld, Ferdinand Hubert Schmitz. Marked: Orivit and the number 2190. Width: 28 cm.

Page 99 centre Biscuit tin with lid, on a plate. Relief ornament of triple-headed rose-blossom. Design and execution by the Orivit pewter works, Cologne-Ehrenfeld, Ferdinand Hubert Schmitz. Marked: Orivit and the number 2125. Diameter of the plate: 19 cm.

Page 99 bottom Biscuit tin with lid. Rippled-line ornament moulded to form a river. Design and execution by the Orivit pewter works, Cologne-Ehrenfeld, Ferdinand Hubert Schmitz. Marked: Orivit and the number 2609. 16 × 16 cm.

clearly. These show up on all factory-produced wares; a way has not yet been found of rendering them invisible. On the whole this defect is barely noticed by the layman; and only a few experts are troubled by it. Special mention should be made of the many different vases and bowls in the display, which even includes complete services.'

Firms and Workshops

'The Aktiengesellschaft (limited share company) 'Orivit' in Cologne-Ehrenfeld must be placed on a par with this firm (i.e. Kayser). Although it has only been manufacturing art pewter for a few years, it has already become the most dangerous rival of the above-mentioned firm. Worth mentioning in particular are the galvanized items, which have been given a superbly clean and even coating'.

'The firms of F. Van Hauten and Son of Bonn, and H. Dautzenberg of Krefeld have also exhibited their wares in this group. The pewterware of the first firm, which is also produced according to system [i.e. *Kayserzinn*], is, to our taste at least, lacking in style. On the other hand, the glass mounts, which are very much in the modern style, are both conceived and executed with

assemblage, burnishing, and polishing are all very cleanly done; and the only blemish is that the stripes left by casting can be seen quite

Candelabrum, c.1903. Examples of
that part of the Jugendstil which
favoured more floral design.
Unknown designers, execution by
the Orivit Company, Cologne-
Ehrenfeld (formerly F.H. Schmitz).
Marked Orivit.

Samovar, c.1900. Russia. No
markings. Height: 35 cm.

great artistry. It is clear that the
firm has focused its attention on
this area, which is perfectly
understandable, considering that it
possesses one of the first glass-
painting works and enjoys a
particularly high reputation as a
decorator of coats of arms,
portraits, etc.
The firm of Dautzenberg, which
has been in existence for a number
of years now, has also exhibited
very fine items, thereby fully
confirming its previous reputation.
These, then, are the principal
exhibitors from our branch in the
'Art' group.....'

'Before we leave the fair Rhine, we
must not forget the only company
producing art pewterware in
Holland, namely the "Urania"
metal products factory in Maestricht.
Lying close to the German border,
this firm was founded some six or
seven years ago. All its models are
originals, designed without exception
by artists of the first rank. The
technical execution may be described
as quite genuinely flawless, regardless of whether one is talking about

gilded, silvered or plain wares. It is
no wonder that Germany is the
firm's principal selling area, since
'Urania' can compete with any
German company; to this end it
maintains two display centres in
Germany, one in Berlin, the other
in Aschen'.

'The largest pewter-producing

left Champagne-cooler, c.1900. This and the following objects are examples of the more austere, geometric designs of the Darmstadt colony. Design by Albin Muller, execution by R. Hardy and Co., Ludenscheid. Marked (on the underside of the base): AM.

below left Full-length mirror, c.1900. The fluid ornamental design of the frame, drawn as if in a single, flowing line, makes this a typical example of the Munich Jugendstil. Design by Richard Riemerschmid, execution by the Osiris works of Walter Scherf & Co., Nuremberg. Marked: Osiris and the number 783.

right Pendulum clock, 1901. The eccentric designer Albin Muller provides a good example here of a tendency characteristic of the Darmstadt colony to monumentalize elements of detail and cover them with lively decoration (mostly coloured). Design by Albin Muller, execution by R. Hardy & Co., Ludenscheid.

establishment in Bavaria is probably the "Isis" Works (previously called "Osiris") in Nuremberg, the property of Walter Scherf and Co. This firm was established at the end of the nineties by recruiting managers and labourers from the "Orivit" company in Cologne. Any visitor to the Bavarian Jubilee Exhibition could have convinced himself of the efficiency of this establishment; furthermore, he will know that it can compete sensibly and on an equal footing with any other enterprise, standing as it does in the forefront of the modern age.'

If the role of pewter as a material had declined in importance in the later years of historicism, then Art Nouveau brought the focus of attention back to its specific material properties. The chief concern was that the shaping and the ornamentation of the pewter object should be attuned to the qualities and the worth of the metal, whilst at the same time ensuring that the object could be produced in large quantities without too much difficulty. The basis of the pewter trade had shifted during the industrial-

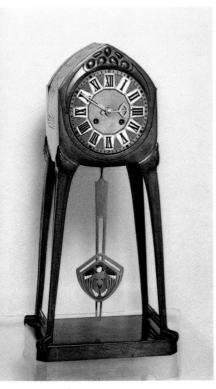

Bavarian Arts and Crafts Exhibition (1902 and 1903), certain well-known artists of the Jugendstil had a most significant impact on pewter and its struggle for new esteem and to win new popularity. Pewter gained a fresh appreciation in Germany thanks above all to the high quality of the designs made by the artists of the Mathildenhohe colony at Darmstadt.

Josef Maria Olbrich, the architect of the Vienna Secession, was the dominant force in the artist's colony founded in 1899 by the last grand duke of Hesse, Ernst Ludwig. In his pewter designs traces can be found of the transition in the Jugendstil towards a style that was severer in conception, sharper in outline, and abjured all elaboration. His jugs and candlesticks tend to be simple forms adorned with flat decoration applied in single flowing lines.

ization process of the nineteenth century from the small craftsman's workshop to series production; this provided outside artists with many commissions to design decorative schemes for pewterware, artists who had not direct contact with the material itself.

Jugendstil artists as pewter designers

Besides those firms listed in the reports of the Arts and Crafts Exhibition in Dusseldorf and the

Peter Behrens developed a logical and linear style in his designs which gave German industrial design a world-wide reputation. **Albin Muller**, on the other hand, exercised his vivid imagination to enliven his pewterware designs by the addition of little ornamental features and the sparing use of colour accentuation. The pewter works of E. Hueck in Ludenscheid gave substance to the ideas of the Darmstadt artists.

right Candelabrum (one of a pair), 1902-1903. The architect of the Darmstadt colony, Joseph Maria Olbrich, also designed, like his contemporaries, small everyday objects. In them he sought a synthesis between a pure two-dimensional effect and a sense of rhythm and movement. The candelabrum displays the bevelled arch-forms to be seen in his architecture, as well as his overriding concern with functionalism. His efforts were directed towards combing structural good sense with pleasing ornamentation. Design by Joseph Maria Olbrich, execution by the Eduard Hueck pewter works, Ludenscheid. No markings. Height: 36 cm.

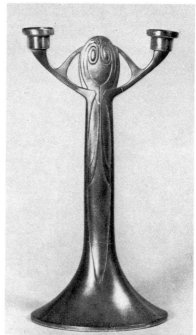

The so-called Deutsche Werkstatten ('German Workshops') opened their own pewter works at Hellerau near Dresden; the most successful pieces were those by **Richard Riemerschmid** and **Wolfgang von Wersin**.

'Kayserzinn'

Among all the enterprises which subscribed to the Jugendstil, pride of place must belong to the firm of Peter Kayser and Son. The Cologne studio of Engelbert Kayser supplied the designs, whilst the Krefeld factory run by Jean (Johann Peter) Kayser handled the mass-production of the wares. The two brothers came from a long-established family of pewterers in Kaiserswerth near Dusseldorf. The products made under the direction

Tureen, 1903. The lively decoration, part relief, part sculpted, seems to have been drawn from a painting by the Norwegian Jugendstil artist Edvard Munch. Design by Aaron Jerndahl, execution by Schroider-Olssen, Stockholm. Marked: Schroider-Olssen and the number 07. Signed: Aaron Jerndahl.

of their father, Johann Peter, had already secured the firm's reputation, to such an extent indeed that the name *Kayser-Zinn* ('Kayser Pewter') had come to be accepted as a trade mark in commercial circles.

By *Kayserzinn* we mean what is sometimes called 'silver tin', a lead-free form of pewter with a long-lasting silvery shine. The description is misleading, in that the metal contains no silver but varying mixtures of copper and antimony. These alloying metals increase the strength of the very soft grain tin and also improve its casting qualities.

'The correct mix for commercial *Kayser-Zinn* must contain at least 8 pounds of copper and antiomony combined, more in the case of particular articles – e.g. for trays, salvers, etc., as much as 12 – 14 pounds. It is strongly recommended to mix some aluminium into the alloy: this makes it tougher and gives it a better shine. Furthermore, the mixture should be smelted down in a boiler rather than a crucible; the latter is an outmoded device and is to be ignored for all practical purposes.' (*Deutsche Zinngiesser*, 15 October 1903)

'The manufacture of *Kayser-Zinn* is no different from any other artistic casting, except that, instead of the so-called 'lost mould' made of sandstone, a metal mould is used.

Initially a plaster core is fashioned according to the artist's ideas and drawings; this has the rough form of the final object. Then the artist begins the modelling in wax; here it is principally a question of allowing the character of the metal to make its effect in the moulds, since no other metal gives such delicate and gentle reliefs or has such a soft and supple shine. 'From the completed model a plaster cast is taken, which is then touched up and to which the finer points are added. It is this new model, complete in all details, which is finally handed over for casting. An iron casting mould naturally requires more effort to work than a sand mould. The individual elements of the metal mould have themselves to be cast from sand moulds and then joined together. Moreover, the skin of the iron is very rough, thus calling for great care on the part of the engraver when touching up.

'The mould is heated up in the same oven and at the same temperature as the casting mass, so that the liquid pewter is responsive to each tiny detail of the modelling. As soon as the molten metal has filled the mould completely, it is 'chilled': the mould is wrapped about with wet cloths, and it is this which gives the pewter its metallic shine and its strength. Large pieces create a certain difficulty in this casting

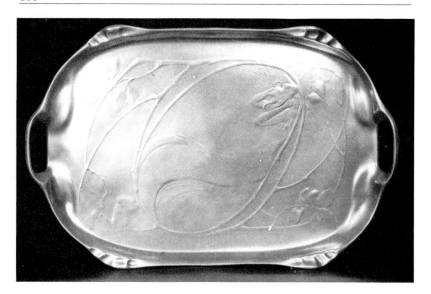

Overleaf Centrepiece, *circa* 1907. At each end of the pointed oval bowl kneels the sculpted figure of a female nude, whose outstretched arms merge into the rim. The square, polished stem with its curved braces supports a circular *bonbon*. A classic example of the fusion of form, ornament, and function. Design by the *atelier* of Engelbert Kayser, Krefeld-Bockum. Marked: oval company stamp and the number 4444. Length: 54 cm; height: 29 cm.

Tray, 1902-1904. On the base a female figure in shallow relief, the lines of her long flowing hair intertwined with the leaves and fruit of rose-twigs. Design by Engelbert Kayser, execution by J.P. Keyser & Son, Krefeld-Bockum. Marked: oval company stamp and the number 4516. Diameter (max.): 49 cm.

(*Deutsche Zinngiesser*, 15 September 1902)

method, since the red-hot iron moulds sometimes weigh several hundredweight and have to be manipulated by means of pulleys and winches.

'The long process of polishing now begins: the metal is passed through acids and scoured with sand to give it that new brightness which sets it apart from every other metal, making it so homelike and thus so well suited to household wares.'

The articles produced by the Kayser company in the complicated processes described above were all part of an ambitious programme whereby well-designed and up-to-date articles used in daily life were to be manufactured in large quantities and made accessible to a broad segment of the consumer population. Vessels were carefully differentiated, many being intended for use only with certain types of

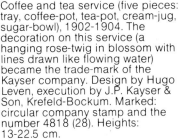

Coffee and tea service (five pieces: tray, coffee-pot, tea-pot, cream-jug, sugar-bowl), 1902-1904. The decoration on this service (a hanging rose-twig in blossom with lines drawn like flowing water) became the trade-mark of the Kayser company. Design by Hugo Leven, execution by J.P. Kayser & Son, Krefeld-Bockum. Marked: circular company stamp and the number 4818 (28). Heights: 13-22.5 cm.

Two vases, c.1905. Both pieces, and especially the two-handled vase with its outline of hanging rose-twig, blossom, and bud, and striking examples of the gentle, fluid dynamic of *Kayser-Zinn* pewterware. Design by the *atelier* of Engelbert Kayser, execution by J.P. Kayser & Son, Krefeld-Bockum. Marked: circular company stamp, the vase on the left bearing the number 4626 and 31, the large vase on the right 4655 and 37. Heights: 30 cm and 38 cm.

dish or drink - e.g. fish and meat dishes, biscuit tins, liqueur jugs; in this way the firm sought to contribute to a more refined table culture.

'In the display in the *Kayser-Zinn* pavilion we find a succession of pieces in pure and pleasing forms that are well suited both to the character of the metal and to the particular type of object. There are complete services, bowls, jugs,

beakers, dishes, jars, tea-pots, coffee-pots, toilette pieces, frames for mirrors and photographs, flower-stands, centrepieces, beautiful candlesticks; we can admire all these pieces and the tasteful way in which they are arranged in the show-cases. And because, for all their artistic merits, they remain solid, down-to-earth articles for everyday use, and not objects designed for a rarefied existence of

Bowl in the shape of a clover-leaf,
c.1900. Form and ornament are
here absolutely one. The stalk of the
clover leaf and thistle is curved to
form a handle on the bowl; in the
hollow sits a bee. Design by the
atelier of Engelbert Kayser, execution
by J.P. Kayser & Son, Krefeld-
Bockum. Marked: oval company
stamp and the number 4098.
Diameter: 24 cm.

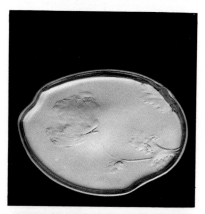

idle pomp and splendour, we can
only wish that we will encounter
them more often, as indications
both of prosperity and of good
taste, in those households where
they are equally welcome whether
as gifts from a friend or purchased
as sound investments.' (*Deutsche
Zinngiesser*, 15 September 1902.)
The relief decoration favoured by
Kayser may be divided into two
groups, orientated respectively
towards the floral and the linear
aspects of Jugendstil ornament.
The first group, which is far and
away the predominant one, is so
heavily influenced in certain
respects by French Art Nouveau

Small tray, with a poppy growing
out of the oval base, 1898-1900.
The piece illustrates the high level
of acomplishment reached by the
Kayser company in its relief pewter.
Design by Hugo Leven, execution
by J.P. Kayser & Son, Krefeld-
Bockum. Marked (on the underside
of the base): oval trade-mark and
the number 4174. Diameters: 19.5
cm. and 24.5 cm.

Ornamental corks, girls' heads,
c.1900.German, unmarked. Heights:
6-7 cm.

that it seems more than likely that
designers from neighbouring France
may also have been active in
Cologne. The form-language is
based on a close affinity with
nature, whence the motifs were
drawn, especially flower and plant

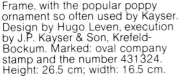

Frame, with the popular poppy ornament so often used by Kayser. Design by Hugo Leven, execution by J.P. Kayser & Son, Krefeld-Bockum. Marked: oval company stamp and the number 431324. Height: 26.5 cm; width: 16.5 cm.

motifs. The object becomes here a plaything of the decoration, completely subordinated to the natural lines and rhythms of a calyx, for example, so that is seems to assume that particular shape. Naked female figures, adapted to the flow of the ornamental line, are an almost indispensable decorative feature.

The free, artistic shaping of surfaces, where linear and floral forms are combined, is a distinctive feature of Japanese graphic art, which had an extraordinarily stimulating effect on the Jugendstil. The aimless, wandering line, derived from nature and determining surface divisions and distribution of mass in the object, is likewise borrowed from Oriental art. Within

such lines, large plant forms unfold on the decorative surface, few in number and with the least attention paid to the illusion of space and to three-dimensional effect, the forms making their impact purely through the boldness and freedom of their contours.

In a number of models the attempt was made to unite form and representation; these can be considered as a special group. Again the idea was derived from nature, so that a vessel might be given the shape of a blossom unfolding; a dragonfly with outspread wings might become a triangular bowl; or a liqueur jug might be designed in the form of a duck, to produce the complete 'natural event'.

The dating and classification of pewterware produced by the Kayser company are made easy for the collector, since every product bears the mark *Kayser-Zinn*, together with a model number cut in bold relief on the underside of the base or foot. These numbers commence in 1895 with the figure 4000 and end in 1909 with 4889. The numbering, however, refers to the year in which the original model was made, and not the year in which the particular piece was cast.

The reputation which *Kayser-Zinn* acquired at the world exhibitions of Paris (1900), Turin and Dusseldorf (1902), and St. Louis (1904) was due not least to the excellence of its designers, men like Hugo Leven, Karl Geyer, Hermann Pauser, Karl Berghoff, and the Dusseldorf painter Johann Christian Kroner.

Firms and workshops

Besides the companies already mentioned we should not forget the firm of F. van Hauten and Son in Bonn, which produced outstanding examples of pewterware with glass mounts. Originally a porcelain and glass colouring works, by the turn of the century it had become one of the leading firms in the pewter business.

In Berlin the firms of Bernhard B. Simon and the Moritz Rosenow Kunst – und Luxuswarenfabrik ('Factory for Art and Luxury

above Three-handled *jardinière*. The handles each show a fully-sculpted bearded man's face. The drawn-in body with its wavy rim is set on a circular sloping base. Execution by J.P. Kayser & Son, Krefeld-Bockum.

above right Writing implements. On the elongated tray, water-lilies with leaves and a dragonfly; the right-hand corner at the back is raised in an arch.

below right Knife rests in the shape of dogs. Besides dachshunds, Kayser also produced knife rests in the form of cats, hares, foxes, and other animals.

Wares') marketed their products under the trade name Wonesor; these had the characteristics of 'silver tin' and were usually given a gold tint.

The firms of F.H. Dautzenberg Jun. and Bitter and Gobbers, both of Krefeld, were also manufacturers of luxury and household pewter, while the Elektra casting works of H. Feith and A. Flock in Cologne produced a number of notable

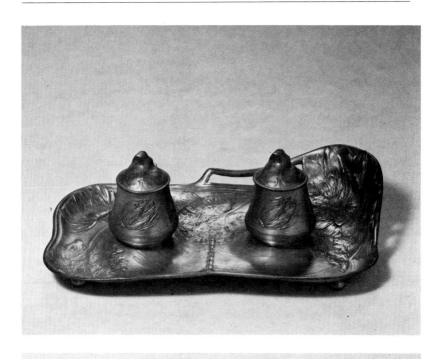

114

above left Sugar-bowl, *c.*1902.
Unknown designer, execution by
J.P. Kayser & Son, Krefeld-Bockum.
Marked (on the underside of the
base): oval factory stamp, the
number 4472, and the letters WZ.
Height: 18.5 cm.

centre Small basket, with four-
stranded handle, *c.*1900. The strands
forming the handle grow out of the
asymmetric bowl in the form of
leaves. Germany, probably J.P.
Kayser & Son, Krefeld-Bockum.
Illegible stamp and number.
Diameter: 29.5 cm.

below Pudding-dish, with cover,
before 1909. On the surface a
stylized, wide-branching cluster of
flowers. The liner of white porcelain
is missing. Design by J.P. Kayser &
Son, Krefeld-Bockum. Marked:
circular company stamp and the
number 4479. Diameter: 22 cm.

above right Pair of candelabra,
*c.*1902. Design by Hugo Leven,
execution by J.P. Kayser & Son,
Krefeld-Bockum. Detail of the
socket and dripping-pan.

pieces in small issues. The pewterware which the metal products factory at Geislingen brought onto the market at the turn of the century was mostly gilded or silvered and soon became a best-seller.

The main pewter manufacturers in Bavaria, in addition to those mentioned earlier in the chapter, were the Orion metal products factory of G.F. Schmitt and the Norica pewter works of Felsenstein and Mainzer.

Karl Gross in Munich produced designs that combine the traditional Bavarian repertory of shapes with spare, flowing Jugendstil ornament. His works were enormously success- ful, but unfortunately there were numerous imitations, not always of high quality. The execution of Gross's conceptions was in the hands of the arts and crafts workshops of Ludwig Lichtinger. Very fine works in the same stylistic trend came from the *ateliers* of the Munich pewterers Ludwig Mory, Josef Schmeidl, de Steinicken & Lohr, and Wilhelm and Lind. Good-quality relief pewter articles were produced by Reinemann & Lichtinger, Nathan Bauernfreund, and Thannhauser Brothers.

French and English pewter around 1900

French pewter at the turn of the century followed in the tradition of that famous master of relief pewter, François Briot; it was bound entirely to the three- dimensional, floral forms of Art Nouveau. Unlike England and Germany, where Britannia metal and 'silver tin', respectively, were used, the pewterware produced in France at this time had a high lead-content and a dark colouring. The most important pewterer in late 19th-century France was Jules Brateau, who created vessels in a comtemporary style with freely- drawn floral ornament. Baffier's pewter is characterized by broad designs and solid decoration; the sweet-pea flower for instance, inspires the shaping of a candlestick, the handle being formed by a serpent licking its way up from the base of the blossom.

Pierre Hoche covers his elaborate vessels with a bright green patina; it is easy to mistake them for ceramic wares. Charpentier's work tends to be florid and highly decorative, yet succeeds in showing the metal's intrinsic properties and merits to excellent advantage.

Because most French Art Nouveau pewter was not produced in series, classification is only possible on the basis of stylistic features; as we

left Ink-well, c.1900. This unmarked object is almost certainly to be ascribed to the Glasgow school. Charles Rennie Mackintosh, the leading figure of this breakaway movement, was developing his distinctive cubical style already in the nineties. The ink-well is a typical example of his 'box-composition', enlivened by an ornamental lattice-work overlay. Unmarked. Height: 18 cm.

below Tray, c.1900. The plain, stretched ornament has been developed from the rounded edges, remaining consistent with the object's function. Design by Archibald Knox, execution by W.H. Haseler, Birmingham. Marketed by Liberty & Co. Marked: Tudric (a designation of English 'fine pewter') and the number 0309.

right Lighter and ashtray, 1903-1904. Design by Albin Müller, execution by the Eduard Hueck pewter works, Ludenscheid. Marked: AM Edelzinn E. Hueck 1848, circular mark.

have tried to indicate, these are sufficiently striking to make this a relatively easy task.

In France the leading firm of silversmiths, L'Orfevrerie Christophle, made pewter objects from the designs of noted Art Nouveau artists. Christophle was the first to introduce galvanization into France; millions of electroplated objects had been produced since 1861. In this process, objects are overlaid by means of electrolysis with a metallic coating. A thin layer of metal, most often silver or gold, is deposited on a base metal, copper, nickel or zinc. The object is put into a plating bath, a mixture containing ions of the precious metal. An electric current is passed through the bath (electrolysis) and a thin layer of the noble metal forms on the galvanized object. At this time Christophle also produced tin-plated zinc objects. Ten parts tin chloride and twenty parts potassium bitartrate are heated with fifty parts of water to complete solution at 50-60°C, the object is dipped in, and finally

above left Candelabrum, *c.*1905. Design and execution by the Isis-Werk, Walter Scherf & Co., Munich and Nuremberg. Marked: Isis and the number 811. Height: 27 cm.

left Hand-mirror, *c.*1900. The plasticity of French Art Nouveau pewter, which rests firmly in the tradition of relief pewter, is clearly to be seen from this example of a hand-mirror. Marked: C. Signed: R. Larabin. Length: 34 cm.

polished to a silvery white shiny surface. In appearance and decoration, the tin-plated objects are always akin to silver work.

England

In England the pewter industry had experienced a huge upturn from the middle of the 19th century, with the result that by around 1900 series manufacture

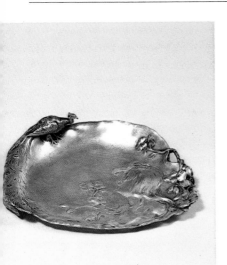

facing right Wine-pitcher, c.1900. The rounded, plastic quality of the ornament is akin to sculpture. The pallid and rather gloomy tone of the metal is typical of French pewter of the period. Design by Antoine Bary. Marked: Etain Garantie.

above Bonbon-dish. The girl's head, cast in relief, is reminiscent of Mucha's delicate female forms, whose yearning poses influenced a whoe generation. Unmarked, France. Diameter: 22 cm.

and long production runs had become common.

Sir Arthur Lasenby Liberty quickly converted the Farmer and Rogers warehouse in Regent Street, London, which he had taken over from his father, into a centre of the trade in arts and *objets d'art*, specializing at first in imports from the Middle and Far East. After founding his own business in 1875, he encouraged English artists to produce designs in the style of Chinese ceramics and Japanese metalwork; this initiated the firm's own unmistakable range of products and fabrics.

Liberty was a close friend of the leading artists of the Arts and Crafts movement and the Guild of Handicraft. The efforts of these groups to improve industrial design and preserve traditional handicrafts had a lasting influence on Liberty. His efforts to embrace all aspects of design, from interior decoration to ceramics and glass, jewellery, printing and bookbinding, fabric design and metalwork, coincide with the aims of the Arts and Crafts movement.

From 1899, Liberty produced silver under the trade name Cymric; in 1902 pewter followed, under the name Tudric.

The execution of the pewter work lay in the hands of the silversmiths W.H. Haseler in Birmingham. The company, which was in existence until 1927, was founded in 1870 by William Haseler and managed from 1896 by his sons William Rabone Haseler and Frank Haseler. The distinctive work commissioned by Liberty made the firm world-famous. Despite the hand-crafted appearance of the pieces, they were produced in large quantities with the help of mechanical techniques, without, however, any ill-effects to their high quality.

The distinctiveness of the Liberty-

Bottle-holder, c.1900. Design and execution by the Norica pewter works of Felsenstein and Mainzer, Nuremberg and Munich. Marked: S.M. 1884 and N. Height: 6.5 cm; diameter: 12 cm.

Butter dish and butter-knife, after 1903. Line and foliage ornament in shallow relief. Design by Archibald Knox, execution by W.H. Haseler, Birmingham. Marketed by Liberty & Co. Marked: Liberty & Co. and the numbers 0163 and 4. Diameter: 13.5 cm.

Haseler pewter objects lies above all in their use of cloisonné enamelling, a technique which had been brought to England by the French ceramic artist Adrien Dalpayrat in 1885. Besides enamelled clock faces, parts of ornaments were picked out in coloured enamel. Liquid transparent enamel was poured into small cells *(cloisons)* made of wire, where it hardened to give a jewel-like appearance. The predominant colouring of Liberty objects - bright turquoise and blue - harmonizes with the dull grey of the pewter.

The designers' names are in most cases not marked on the pieces. Nevertheless, they were the best free-lance English designers - e.g. Jessie M. King, Archibald Knox and Rex Silver - working under the influence of Christopher Dresser. Dresser had set himself the task of producing simple designs economical in material, and in decoration logically related to the object.

The ornamentation of the Liberty Tudric pieces is two-dimensional, with light, occasionally lively lines linked to strange, delicate stylized flowers leading a decorative life of their own on the thinnest of stems.

Covered pitcher, with handle bound in raffia, 1903. The classic form of the covered pitcher is here given an Art Nouveau variation. Design by Archibald Knox, execution by W.H. Haseler, Birmingham.

Bonbon dish, with glass inset, 1903.
Design by Archibald Knox, execution
by W.A. Haseler, Birmingham.
Marketed by Liberty & Co. Marked:
Tudric (trade name) and W. and the
number 0276. Height: 17 cm.

Scotland - Glasgow

On the edge of the English scene,
in Scotland, a group of artists
formed the Glasgow Group, under
the leadership of the architects
Charles Rennie Mackintosh and
Herbert McNair and their wives,
the Macdonald sisters. The
rectilinear forms of Mackintosh's
designs already anticipate the
Functionalism of the twenties.
The more figurative ornamentation
of Frances and Margaret Macdonald
derives its basic conception and
details of its motifs directly from
the Pre-Raphaelites. They designed
embroideries, fabrics, jewellery,
painted wall panels and hammered
metalwork, especially pewter objects
with coloured enamel and glass
inserts.

The frail, elongated figures, merging into the non-representational, pass over into a belated mannerism. The forms are ghost-like, scarcely capable of supporting their small, segmented heads, and everything about them tends to ornament: the folds of their robes, the flowers in their heads and hands.

Outside the classic pewter-manufacturing nations of England, France and Germany, we find only isolated examples of Art Nouveau pewterware, made to suit prevailing local tastes.

Vienna

In Vienna the Wiener Werkstatte produced severe, rectilinear pewter vessels, combining new, unconventional design with a demand for practicality and suitability.

The group saw its chief field of activity as the decoration and furnishing of houses. In the rooms and interiors they designed, everything formed a conceptual unity, from flowertubs and banisters to furniture, to carpets, wall-hangings and electrical fittings.

The head of the organization, Josef Hoffman, designed simple cylindrical pewter articles divided into fields of delicate small-scale decoration. His preference for cubic ornament earned him the nickname 'Brettl-Hoffmann'. At the same time, in direct contrast to Hoffmann the designers Koloman Moser and Dagobert Peche produced metalwork of stylized, rhythmic design.

Netherlands

The leading Dutch designer of the turn of the century was the jeweller Jan Eisenloffel, who had studied with Josef Hoffmann at the Wiener Werkstatte.

From 1902 - after working at first predominantly in silver - he worked by preference in copper, brass and pewter. His containers, pots and cups, of simple, practical form, were models of modern utensils. Eisenloffel showed that austerity of form and elegance were not mutually exclusive and that a severe ornamental style can have the same lively effect as a complicated floral one.

The manufacturer of Art Nouveau pewter found himself confronted with a problem which he shared with all artists of the movement; it was well formulated in the *Deutsche Zinngiesserzeitung* in 1907: 'For the time being it must also be the natural task of the manufacturer to educate the purchasing public by offering it forms that are both artistically and technically impeccable, so helping it to a mature evaluation of artistic forms; this is a task which is really rather difficult in some respects, since the purchasing public still chooses to indulge in all manner of lapses of taste.'

The Beginning of Modern Pewter Design

Industrial product versus handicraft

The twenties, known as 'a decade of contrasts', were marked by a radical upheaval throughout the whole area of arts and crafts. On the one hand, we find luxury items of an almost crazy extravagance, produced for a society between the wars that was forever hankering after novelty and seeking pleasure in wild excess. On the other hand, there arose a movement which deliberately adapted itself to the demands and the possibilities created by a mass society and its new technology, seeking in this the basis for new artistic standards.

In 1925 the largest Arts and Crafts Exhibition of the twenties opened in Paris. The *Exposition Internationale des Arts Décoratives et Industrielles Modernes* was a small town in itself, in which a great many countries participated. There were two important exceptions, however: Germany and the United States. The reasons for Germany's absence are familiar enough: after long deliberations by the relevant authorities the invitation was eventually issued too late for a comprehensive picture of the German arts and crafts scene to be assembled for display. Thus the exhibition, in spite of its scale, represented a part only of the whole picture, since neither the artists of the Weimar Bauhaus nor those of De Stijl in Holland - two absolutely seminal movements - were represented.

In Liepzig in 1927 a similar exhibition was held, but this did not arouse the same world-wide interest as the Paris exhibition. If the exhibits from France are considered, then the impression given is that only the individual works of a small number of artists achieved a high standard, whereas the industrial products and the mass of craftsmen-made items show a serious decline in quality - unlike those produced in Germany and elsewhere. They are certainly attractive objects, in fantastic shapes and extravagant colour-schemes; but they carry no deeper resonance.

A further capitulation to the taste of the bourgeoisie was not, however, deemed appropriate in the midst of the post-war years. If the Jugendstil was a manifesto of the bourgeoisie, then the twenties, in the guise of Art Deco, was its last flowering. In Germany and Scandinavia, on the other hand,

Pewter bowl and saucer, 1929. Whereas in previous centuries pewter was only rarely worked with a hammer, this technique has become increasingly common since the twenties. Design by Professor von Wersin, execution by K. Riepl. Unmarked. Diameter: 14 cm.

Tea service (four pieces: tray, tea-pot, cream-jug, sugar-bowl), in 1912. In the first decade of this century the Jugendstil gradually turned away from luxury objects to more functional, everyday wares. Design by Richard Riemerschmid, execution by the Deutsche Werkstatten. Unmarked. Heights: 4.2-13 cm.

Tea-caddy and biscuit-tin, 1933 and 1927/28. Oval tea-caddy in the shape of a water-bottle, design by Richard Wiedermann, execution by Eugen Wiedermann, Regensburg. Marked: 'fine metal' mark featuring a pot and E.W.
Rectangular tin, design by Professor Hillerbrand, Deutsche Werkstatten. Marked: DW. Heights: 9 cm and 4.8 cm.

fresh developments *were* taking place; here plans were being made for the future, and designs produced which are still with us today.

Workshop and studio communities

Many associations had been established to tackle the question of new forms in the applied arts, some as early as the turn of the century. The theoretical programmes they published give a clear indication of the new trend. The following extract from Hermann Obrist's pamphlet 'Functional or

fanciful' elucidates the tasks which the Munich Secession had set itself:

'It is clear to all of us that a healthy folk tradition in the handicrafts can only obtain if the forms that are used are simple, straightforward, practical, and absolutely functional. It is also clear to us that all parties to this matter, including the artists, must work towards a realization of this lost ideal.'

left Tea-pot, 1931. Design by Professor von Wersin. Execution by Max Oblatter, Munich. Marked: 'angel fine metal mark', Mo and Handarbeit ('handmade'). Height 11 cm.

above Tea-pot, with ebony handle, 1930. Design and execution by Swenskt Tenn, Stockholm.

United Workshops for Arts and Crafts

In 1905 the artists' association known as the Vereinigte Werkstatten in Kunst und Handwerk ('United Workshops for Arts and Crafts') was founded. Peter Behrens and Richard Riemerschmid were the principal artists to work with pewter and create a variety of objects in the light of traditional forms used by the craftsmen of old. In 1907 Peter Behrens was appointed artistic adviser to the giant electrical company AEG in Berlin. In his person we can see the transition being made from the artist working for an elite to the designer of a respectable, well-conceived commercial art.

For all its efforts this movement in the arts and crafts towards a new, down-to-earth art took a long time to find acceptance. No doubt it was the general fear of forfeiting what was 'pleasant' and 'comfortable' that made it so hard for the modern movement to gain a foothold; it was conveniently forgotten that the concept of 'comfort' is one that changes with the times, and that consequently our sense of what is comfortable

Two small bowls and a small jar, 1930. The gadrooned ornament is very finely executed. Design and execution (all three pieces) by Svenskt Tenn, Stockholm. Marked: Svenskt Tenn, Stockholm T8. Heights: 4-7 cm.

and homely will hardly coincide with that of our grandfathers.

Bauhaus

The name Bauhaus is inextricably linked with the search for innovation in the arts. This art institute was founded in 1919 by the architect Walter Gropius in Weimar, when he combined the local Academy of Arts with the School of Arts and Crafts.
The aims of the institute were formal clarity, objectivity and functionalism, the defeat of historicism, and the assimilation of the object to new forms of technology. All the fine arts were included; the individual disciplines were divided into classes and workshops, each presided over by a 'Bauhaus master'.

De Stijl

De Stijl was a movement established in Holland in 1918; its formal characteristics, as seen in its designs, are abstraction, a strong favouring of the straight line and the rectangle, and the division of surfaces into vertical and horizontal elements.

Scandinavia

Throughout Scandinavia the modern movement established itself with the minimum of resistance. The Stockholm Exhibition in 1930 showed clearly that in the Scandinavian countries, too, recourse to historical styles was now at last a thing of the past. Pewterware from Stockholm, very well designed and executed, gradually captured new markets all over Europe.

Most of these works were in fact unique, although they could have been used as models for series production.

The pewter made in this period has something of an elitist image,

derived to a large extent from the perfection of its execution and the precision with which the hardness of the metal is gauged and exploited. What was seen then as an example to be followed should today have become an accepted reality; for as well as conserving the pewter of past ages it is important to create space and opportunity for original, progressive design.

Three tea-caddies, 1931, 1925 and 1925. Three typical examples of the synthesis between functionalism and an ornamental scheme based on certain set forms. Tea-caddy with horizontal fluting, design by Pathy Kreuther, student of the Nuremberg School of Applied Arts. Marked: EW and 'fine metal' mark featuring a pot. Centre: Tea-caddy, design by Wolfgang von Wersin, Deutsche Werkstatten, Hellerau. Marked: DW. Tea-caddy with diamond lattice, design by Wolfgang von Wersin, Deutsche Werkstatten, Hellerau. Marked: DW. Heights: 11.5-13.5 cm.

Information for the collector

Collectors of pewter can be divided into two groups: those who acquire objects simply for their aesthetic qualities; and those who build up a more systematic collection on an historical, technical, or formal basis.

The first group has existed ever since the second half of the sixteenth century when collecting became the pastime of aristocratic circles and of the well-to-do bourgeoisie. In this age of display pewter the function of a particular article had long since lost its primary importance, and it was seen rather as a showpiece, a piece of pure ornament.

In the mid-nineteenth century the awakening interest in historical links, together with a rapidly growing trend towards art-historical research, led to the first comprehensive and systematic collections of pewter.

For the individual it is clear, therefore, that both the starting-point and the motivation for an active involvement with pewter can vary greatly. The following points of information will nevertheless be of interest to both groups.

Pewter as a material

Pewter possesses a certain value simply as a material and may be found in varying states. Apart from the different forms of ornamentation pewter has a specific kind of 'decoration' derived from the alloy that is used; hence it can have a dull, grey-black surface, or a warm, soft glow, or a silvery shine. It is a matter simply of personal taste which of these the collector prefers.

The appearance of the metal is also a question of quality, since pewter alloys with a high lead content possess a much lower *material* value than those containing copper or antimony. The significance of the mixing ratio is seen clearly in the strict regulations regarding alloys enforced by the Pewterer's Company.

Knowledge of material and technique

Many wrong decisions will be avoided if the collector has not only decided clearly on a particular type of pewter, but also possesses a good knowledge of the material and the techniques involved in its preparation. An exact knowledge of technical processes will enable him to recognize quality instantly, and quite independently of external appearance. If a truly objective judgement on quality is to be made, regardless of attributions and dealers' assurances, then he must know, for instance, how a well-executed piece of relief or engraved decoration should appear. Besides a feeling for beauty and the balance of form, the collector also needs as wide a technical knowledge as possible.

Nature and style of a collection

Someone starting a collection will need to decide first of all on a guiding focus. As a rule, collections are not general and unlimited in scope, but circumscribed by geographical, historical, formal, or stylistic considerations. All kinds of motives may be crucial in determining the area in which a collection is to be formed. One person may collect the pewterware of a particular period, such as the eighteenth century or the Art Nouveau epoch; another tries to acquire as many pieces as possible from a particular geographical area; others still may concentrate on relief pewter, on engraved objects, hollow-ware, guild pewter, kitchen utensils, apothecary vessels, articles with specific motifs (e.g. representations of miners), or on marks

and touches. (There are some collectors who are content to have the mark on its own, cut out of the object.) Then, finally, there are those collectors (probably, in fact, the majority) who direct their attentions in the first instance towards beauty of form and ornament and towards the possible historical importance of a piece.

Much can be collected within an overall, logical context. The sooner a collector has made up his mind as to the theme of his collection, the quicker he can create something that is serious, personal and worthwhile.

Opportunism and individualism

He should take further care not to be unduly influenced by the tides of fashion nor by 'lucky opportunities'. Personal preference should always play an important role in collecting, however esoteric, when all is said and done, a sheer liking for the object is still the best precondition for a good choice.

The current state of knowledge

Once the 'motto', so to speak, of the collection has been determined, then the beginner must turn his thoughts to methods of collecting.

First of all, he must acquire as much practical knowledge of pewter as possible. To do this is no onerous task, but an unadulterated pleasure, as any collector will soon realize. To have all the facts concerning an acquired object in his head is an essential element of 'collector's delight'.

It soon becomes apparent just how important publications are, since published pieces will have a higher market value by virtue of their comparability. It is a good idea to subscribe to the relevant catalogues at a specialist bookdealer; in this way, the collector can find out what has appeared on the international front in terms of specialist literature. Any exhibition, any book, may illustrate and describe pieces which he has in his own collection.

As in any other area, a certain 'training' period is necessary before someone can be described as a 'complete' collector. A tiny initial interest can blossom into true connoisseurship by the careful study of specialist literature and an alert eye for anything appearing in print on the subject of pewter.

Further advice and information can be found in new and second-hand bookshops, in libraries, museums especially local and folk museums, and private collections.

Marks and autographs

The value of a piece of pewter cannot be measured simply on the basis of its markings, since fakes have to be reckoned with in some areas. For this reason special attention should be paid to the section on fakes and imitations.

The overall impression, the state of preservation, and the quality of workmanship - these are all criteria that are as equally important in determining authenticity as are marks, stamps, and autographs. This in no way diminishes the primary importance of the latter features for purposes of identif-ication.

Art object and mass-produced article

The problem of mass-produced wares versus unique *objets d'art* is not one that centres on quality in the case of pewter; alongside so-called 'display pewter', pewterware for general, everyday purposes has always been made that can be called 'mass-produced'. It would be nonsense to ignore the latter, since it is only with the help of these simple, everyday articles that an adequately representative collection can be assembled. And it must be remembered that in the course of the centuries a great deal of pewterware has been lost, due to various causes: constant use and natural attrition; trade in old pewter; tin disease; metal requis-itioning in wartime; inadequate storage conditions; insufficient

knowledge of the subject.
These factors have all contributed to contemporary recognition of the fact that high-quality everyday pewter possesses true artistic merit, if only on account of its scarcity.

Tin disease

If tin is subject to extreme cold, it can turn into a grey coloured powder - grey tin - a fact which had already been observed in antiquity. 'Except on a few warm days, our whole world of pewter is in variable transformation, in other words in a metastable condition, so that the pewterware which we use in our daily lives has the tendency to change to a powdery grey modification' (Prof. Ernst Cohen).

At room temperature this process takes of course a very long time; if, on the other hand, common tin is brought into contact with grey tin, then the process is accelerated. The grey tin has a contagious effect, hence the name 'tin pest' given to this phenomenon. Tin pest sets in as a small, barely visible black point and leads eventually to the total decomposition of the object. This disease also occurs in abnormally damp conditions, but it is to all intents and purposes ruled out in most pewterware on account of the lead and antimony it contains. (Even at

$- 40°C$ the presence of antimony in pewter can extend the transformation to more than five years.)

By treating the metal with appropriate counteracting acids in the early stages of the disease, it is possible to put a stop to the process of decomposition, or at the least, to slow it down. If, however, the proper amount of care and attention is given to pewter, then there is little danger of it contracting tin pest, particularly as the more even room temperatures found in houses today precludes the necessary cold and damp.

Scale may also form as a result of corrosion; in the course of years it will spread out over the whole surface in large patches.

Fakes

The problem of fakes is one that is familiar to every art lover and collector. Fakes, often produced with great skill and refinement, are always hard to detect.

Besides the obvious need for a thorough knowledge of the historical and stylistic background, there are a number of specific practical tips which are indispensable aids to establishing authenticity.

Already in the nineteenth century

the instances of pewter forgery were numerous. The pewterers of the time thought nothing of making replicas of Gothic or Renaissance pieces, but profiteers gave them an apparently genuine patina and sold them on the market as originals. This patina was achieved quite simply by rubbing garlic or lampblack into the surface; for particularly subtle effects butter of antimony (anhydrous antimony chloride) was used. Nowadays an 'antique' patina is achieved mainly by using dilute solutions of nitric acid, hydrochloric acid, antimony chloride, powdered alum, and sulphuric acid. In these cases the collector is fairly safe, since by applying citric acid he can distinguish between the false patina, which is affected by the acid, and the genuine patina, which remains undamaged. An abrasive may be used as an alternative to citric acid.

Dents, scratches, and other minor injuries can all indicate genuineness to the collector, although even these must be checked carefully in case they turn out to be 'wear and tear' added at a later date. Signs of attrition, caused by real age or heavy use, should logically only appear in those parts of the vessel subjected to the greatest strain. Faked damage often looks too even or else is found in areas where it could not possibly have occurred

had the object been in long and steady use.

Nor are marks themselves necessarily a guarantee, since the more able forgers have made a point of acquiring old punches or making their own, and have used these to stamp their fakes. Imitation stamps can be detected in two ways. Firstly, the surface features of a piece are often worn down, whereas the marks still look fresh and sharply cut, having suffered little exposure. Secondly, the stylistic characteristics of the piece often do not accord with the touchmark: either place and time do not correspond, or else mediocre pieces carry marks that are incompatible with their quality. Care is advised even when dealing with old marks, since original touches are often soldered onto new wares in the same way as are bases, handles, and lids.

Copies of *relief* pewter are especially common. The forging method is a simple one: a plaster cast is made according to the original sand mould. Experience will tell, however, from the surface of an object whether it has been cast in a stone, bronze, or iron mould, or whether it has been made from a sand or plaster mould taken from worn-out originals. In the latter case the surface of the replica will be blurred and coarse-grained; it will also be porous and contain little holes which form as a result of air pockets during the casting.

There are other ways in which a piece may be exposed as a fake: where the casting burs and pins have been treated carelessly; where the metal has blotches looking like cloud-patches; or where the outlines of cut or engraved work are indistinct.

A chemical analysis of alloying ratios provides a further means of checking a piece of pewter. Fakes often have a high lead-content (to increase the profit margin); this also makes them lighter, depriving them of the proper 'feel'.

Identification is more difficult in the case of so-called 'half-fakes'. These include added inscriptions (inscriptions, for example, engraved in the eighteenth or nineteenth centuries onto good pewter of the seventeenth century), and pewter-ware that has been made more 'valuable' by adding decoration. This category also includes articles which have been assembled from various parts belonging to older pieces.

The history of forgeries is as old as the working of pewter itself. Almost everything has been, and still is, copied. The collector should not be disheartened by this, for a love of pewter is soon followed by a feeling for its genuineness. And the practical suggestions offered above should prevent any severe miscalculations.

The care and restoration of pewter

A layer of dark oxide will form easily on a pewter surface as a result of chemical pollutants in the atmosphere, especially in our cities. Both public and private collectors have sought to prevent such oxidization by covering the freshly cleaned surface with a thin film of transparent lacquer, but they have found that a nylon-based lacquer affects the substance of an object; it is therefore not to be recommended. A more advisable, if more laborious, way is to *clean* pewter from time to time.

Cleaning pewter is not to be confused with polishing it. It is true that a hard, bright shine can be achieved by the rotating action of electric polishing wheels passed rapidly over a pewter surface, but such a shine is not consistent with the material nor with the craftsman's original intentions.

Pieces that do not carry relief work can be cleaned using horsetail (*equisetum*) and suds (or grain tin), a process still to be recommended today for flat surfaces. Pewter with a high lead-content can be cleaned by immersion in dilute hydrochloric acid; this must be done with extreme care, since this dangerous liquid can cause substantial damage to object and collector.

Relief pewter should only be treated with plain soap suds or with a very soft brush. Dirt that has lodged in hollows, recesses, and other awkward places can be taken off with a varnish-remover, as can any traces of nicotine. It should be applied to a section of the object at a time and then rubbed off with a cloth.

Where pewter has been poorly kept and the surface has become thin, corroded, porous, or patinated, special care is required when cleaning; in such cases this is probably best left to an experienced restorer.

In the cleaning process it is important that the *natural* patina of the pewter remains unaffected. This patina gives the surface a grey or grey-black colouring, without being of any perceptible substance itself, like rust on iron or verdigris on brass. Thus it does not cause any substantive change to the object, but rather stains it, and in a manner which, far from detracting from its appearance, is much

discussed and admired.

Repairs should also be entrusted to a proven expert; a restorer's workshop is the best place for objects which have developed pores, cracks, or dents, and for objects which have been bent, cracks, or dents, and for objects which have been bent out of shape or whose handles or bases have come loose; here they can be filled, patched up, soldered, and made good.

Again, it is the professional restorer who should be left to treat 'tin pest'. The treatment is long and laborious, and success cannot be guaranteed in every case. The affected areas are scraped out and rubbed down, after which the object is boiled in a solution of water and hydrochloric acid. This is followed by an extended water bath to ensure that the acid has been rinsed off.

Glossary

The following are some of the
terms that the collector may expect
to encounter either in the literature
on the subject, or in dealers' and
auctioneers' catalogues.

Aberdeen: A type of Scottish wine
measure, often unlidded.

Akerne: Old English form of
acorn, and used to describe the
rounded knop found on spoons,
particularly of the fifteenth
century.

Alienated: Formerly in the
possession of the Church and now
in secular hands. Such ecclesiastical
ware could not, technically, be
transferred from sacred used
without a formal permission or
Faculty, but a great deal of ware
(both pewter and other materials)
was passed over in the eighteenth
and nineteenth centuries, probably
without such permission.

Ashberry: A pewter alloy
containing a high percentage of
antimony. It was much used in
Georgian times for items such as
buckles that had to withstand hard
wear: it is also considerably
brighter and more silvery than true
pewter.

Assay: In pewter terms, not just
the act of testing the quality of a

metal but the actual measure used,
normally a ball of standard alloy,
which could be compared with a
ball of the same shape and size of
the alloy under test. Differences in
weight would disclose errors or
fraud in the test alloy.

Baluster: Used to describe the
characteristic 'pot bellied' shape of
English measures, that swell out
above the base then taper to a
narrow neck.

Bennett's book: A register,
compiled by John Bennett, Master
of the Company of Pewterers in
1679, of the Liverymen and
Yeomen of the Company. This
valuable record, which adds to the
Company's own lists, is in the
possession of the Worshipful
Company of Pewterers.

Beefeater: A type of flagon. The
name derives, apparently, from the
similarity between the design of
the lid and the headgear worn by
the Yeomen of the Guard, now the
Warders of the Tower of London.

Billies and Charleys: Early
nineteenth century fakes. Billy

Typical bottle shapes:

1-4 German screw-top bottles
  5 German screw-top bottle
  6 Lathe-turned screw-top bottle
  7 Hexagonal screw-top bottle
  8 Powder flask

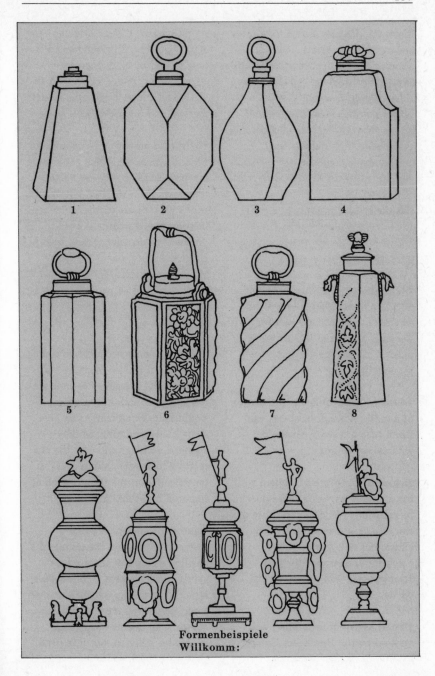

Formenbeispiele
Willkomm:

137

Smith and Charley Eaton, pewterers in London at the time, made a number of fake ecclesiastical seals and badges, some of which, it was claimed, were excavated when London Bridge was being rebuilt. These curious objects, considerably larger than the originals they imitate, have a certain naive charm, and are collected in their own right.

Bismuth: Like antimony, a metal added to pewter alloys as a hardener. Up to 3% was permissible in plate alloys.

Black-metal: An alloy of three-fifths tin to two-fifths lead: it was as a result particularly soft for working, and, from its use in making organ pipes, is known as pipe metal.

Boss: A raised dome in the centre of a plate. Bossed, however, can mean with a convex centre, not with an actual boss.

Brassed: Decorated or inlaid with brass. As brass was a more durable metal, a brass edge to the base or rim of a vessel, such as a dairy churn, not only gave a more colourful appearance but also strengthened and protected the whole.

Broad arrow mark: The mark applied by the Pewterers Company to inferior or false work.

Paradoxically, though originally a sign of poor quality, the mark is now valued by collectors because of its scarcity, since much of such work would have been confiscated, marked and melted down.

Britannia metal: A compound of tin and antimony, which could be machine worked and was harder than pewter. In the mid-nineteenth century over one hundred factories in and around Sheffield were producing this ware. Traditionally Britannia metal has been ignored by pewter collectors, but the ware does form part of pewter's history and is a source for Victorian design and forms.

Capacity seal: A punchmark or seal applied by the Inspector of Weights and Measures to indicate the approved quantity a vessel would hold. Such marks can give some guide to dating, as they changed with variations in the law relating to weights and measures, for example on the introduction of Imperial Measures in 1826.

Castor-oil spoon: A piece of medical equipment, consisting of a bowl, in which the oil could be gently warmed, with a hollow pipe attached to the lip whereby the oil could be poured into the patient's mouth. The overall shape thus resembles a spoon, but it is used, as it were, back to front.

Cawdle cup: A cup or bowl with two handles. Cawdle, or caudle (the latter being the more modern spelling) was a drink of gruel, ale or wine mixed with spices and served to invalids.

Changed-touch: Like the broad arrow mark, a sign of fraud or poor workmanship. A pewterer who persistently offended would be asked to surrender his punches and be given a special touch, often a double f. Pieces with such marks are rare.

Chasing: A form of decoration made by a punch or lining tool, which indents the metal (as opposed to engraving, where metal is removed during the decorative process, either by a burin or by acid.)

Chopin: A measure of six gills (1½ pints), derived probably from the French *chopine*, and used specifically of Scottish measures for spirit or wine.

Coaster: A small round tray or stand for a decanter, vessel or bottle.

Coffin-pieces: Pewter copies of ecclesiastical ware, which were made during the thirteenth century to be buried in the coffin of a priest.

Cologne flagon: A design for a flagon or measure with a domed lid and raised foot and exaggerated baluster.

Cri: The tinny sound given off by tin and pewter when bent backwards and forwards. However, it is not an infallible guide since some alloys, especially ones containing antimony, do not give off this slight but characteristic sound.

Cruets: Sacramental vessels for the wine and water for Communion or Mass.

Cupping dish: A surgical vessel, used to catch the blood let from the patient, and so sometimes found with gradations.

Date letters: Hallmarks found on silver to indicate the year of manufacture. Such marks were not made on English pewter, but some Scandinavian pieces do carry them.

Double handle: A handle in the shape of a reversed 'S' resting on a 'C'.

Ecuelle: The French word for a bowl or porringer.

Engraving: A form of decoration achieved by cutting into the metal with a burin or sharp tool.

Essay-piece: The object submitted to the Court by an apprentice wishing to be released from his identures.

Facet: Diamond shape panels used as decorative surfaces on German ware.

Feast-vessel: Dishes, chargers and bowls so called because they were hired out for use at feasts and banquets.

Fillet: A thin beading around the rim of a piece, both for decoration and to add strength to the whole, since the fillet would be cast with the piece.

Gadroon: A form of decorative design in which curved lines radiate from a central point.

Garnish: A complete service of pewter flatware, normally being a dozen each of platters, dishes and small plates.

Guernsey measure: A distinctive type of Channel Islands measure.

Gut: A pewter vessel for cooling wine.

Hammered: Part of the process of working pewter, used by craftsmen to give extra strength to a piece, and particularly used for spoons. It should not necessarily show as a finish on the ware.

Hanseatic: Work from the area around Bremen, Lubeck and Hamburg, and specifically the flagons produced in the late medieval period around there.

Hanap: A drinking vessel, of Dutch or German origin, elaborately decorated and often for guild use.

Harvester: A shape of measure, also called haystack, peculiar to Irish pewter, and named for its resemblance to the conical hay-stacks found in Southern Ireland.

Hawksbill: A ewer of considerable capacity, sometimes with a spout for pouring.

Hollow-ware: The general name for pots, flagons and tankards. *c.f.* sadware.

Typical flagon shapes:
1 Hanseatic flagon
2 Danish flagon
3 Cologne flagon
4 Baluster flagon
6 Bohemian flagon
7 Flagon on a foot
8 Franconian flagon
9 French wine pitcher
10 Glockenkanne
11 Lirlkanne
12 Arabesque flagon

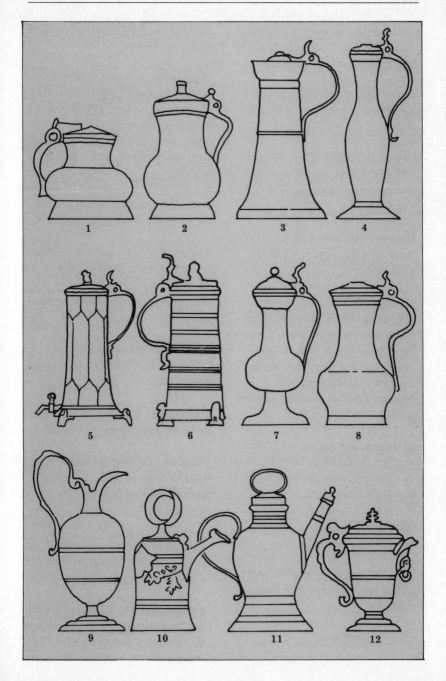

Jan Steen: Name for a distinctive spouted flagon, frequently illustrated in the Dutch artist's paintings.

Kayzerzinn: German pewter manufacturer from the Art Nouveau period.

Lay metal: An alloy of 20% tin to 80% lead. Thus lay men are pewterers who particularly used this alloy.

Loggerhead: Shape for an inkstand with a flat disc forming the base.

London mark: Unlike the silver hall-marks, which show the assay office, there were no place marks for pewter. The X or Rose and Crown mark, a mark showing high or export standard ware, is however referred to as the London mark.

Maidenhead: A knop in the form of a female figure or bust, which is so called because the form represents the Virgin.

Mistery: The craft or guild of pewterers.

Montpellier: Pewter alloy found in Europe, with only 10% lead content.

Mull: A snuff box.

Mutchkin: A Scottish measure, of about ¾ of a pint.

Noggin: In general a small pot that holds under half a pint, and, also, when speaking of Irish measures, the concave-shaped measure that only holds ¼ gill, and. so is the smallest normal size in a set.

Pale: Inferior, soft solder, used in repair work, also called peak.

Patina: Normally the fine, mellow smooth surface of pewter, the result of care and polishing. Alternatively, patinated can mean corroded or oxidized.

Pied-de-biche: A type of spoon which has the end split into two, as a deer's foot.

Planishing: A process of hardening metal by hammering.

Pointillé: Decorated by punching holes with a fine point. A form of decoration often found on the rim of plates.

Porringer: A shallow dish with flat ears or handles projecting from the sides, used for serving porridge.

Posset: A drink of hot milk which has been curdled by adding wine or ale, and often flavoured with nutmeg. Hence a posset-cup.

Pewter marks

There was rarely a legal obligation to mark pewter (unlike silver) but the guilds both in England and Europe made particular efforts to maintain standards and protect their members by insisting that pewter be marked by the maker. A selection of pewter marks, English, German and other, is here given to show the range - and invention - of such touches, which often make a pun or rebus on the maker's name. A full catalogue of the English touches is available in books by Cotterell and Massé (see the bibliography that follows).

The mark of Robert Lucas, Master of the Pewterers' Guild, 1667. This is the first touch on the plates at Pewterers' Hall.

The device of a cardinal's hat, together with the initials P.P., suggests this is the mark of Peter Priest, who became a Yeoman of the Company in 1667.

The mark of William Vinmont, dated 1678. The pillar and thistle are common devices on pewter marks.

The mark of Thomas Falconer, or Faulkner, shows a hawk and crown and the date 1679.

Henry Adams, Pickadilly (*sic*), entered his touch in 1686.

Thomas Smith chose to use his touch to advertise his wares, and so included a tankard in the design he struck in 1682.

Pounce-boxes: Containers for pounce (pumice or find sand). This material was used both to prepare the writing surface and to blot letters, being sprinkled on to the surface from a pounce-box, which thus resembles a pepperpot, save in that the lids and bases were more accessible, as the unused pounce would be put back in.

Pricket: A type of candlestick which has a spike in the place of a socket for the candle.

Purchase: The part that allows one to grip or lift a lid, thus the thumbpiece.

Queen's Metal: A variant of Britannia metal, alloying tin with antimony, copper and bismuth, used during the Victorian era.

Reeded-edge: A form of decoration applied to plates and dishes in which a series of bands runs parallel to the rim. Thus single-reeded, where there is but one band.

Repoussé: Relief decoration in which the design is hammered into the metal from the reverse side.

Sadware: Dishes, chargers and other flatware, as opposed to hollow-ware.

Saler: A salt container, (also spelt salier, the old french word for a salt).

Seal: The mark put onto the side or lip of a measure by an inspector, that confirms the quantity it can contain.

Silvorum: Imitation silver. Used by pewterers in the seventeenth century in particular to make spoons, a market where there was considerable rivalry with the silversmiths.

Spinning: A process whereby hollow-ware can be made from a flat sheet by pressure on a lathe over a wooden core. The process was not much used in traditional pewter making, but came into vogue with the development of mechanical lathes in the nineteenth century. The process was of course much used in the manufacture of Britannia metal.

Stake: A pewtermaking tool, made of hardwood and used for moulding curves by hammering.

Standish: A stand to contain ink, pens and other writing materials.

Stubenkanne: A ceremonial flagon.

Tappit-hen: A word used to describe the traditional shape of Scottish measure, with its charact-eristic cylindrical top and fluted

I. Savidge's mark, struck on the plate in 1678, shows his allegiance to London, for it is supposed that the figures on either side of the bell represent Gog and Mogog, the giants whose effigies stood in the Guildhall.

Thomas Buttery, whose mark is dated 1693, chose to make a play only on his initial, when he used a bee as his device.

The same idea was used by Timothy Fly, who became a Yeoman in 1710.

The lion of England and the pavillion shown on Charles Cranley's touch are in fact the arms of the Merchant Taylor's Company.

A pewter mark often also carried the pewterer's place of work, such as William Fasson's touch for 1752. There are records of several pewterers with the surname Fasson, and it seems likely that the trade passed from father to son in the same family.

The Hammermen of Edinburgh also kept records of their members' touches: Thomas Inglis worked there in the first third of the eighteenth century. The various marks allowed for use on items of different size.

Pewter was also made in Ireland, as Martin Merry's mark shows. The right hand mark also has the X sign for quality or export ware. Martin Merry was working around 1825.

waist. The term properly refers to
the quantity the vessel held (three
pints Imperial or one Scottish pint)
and the name may be derived from
the French *Topynette* or quart, or
from 'tapped' or crested.

Temper: An alloy of tin and
copper.

Touch: The term for a pewterer's
mark. Thus, touch-plate, the sheets
of pewter kept as records at
Pewterer's Hall, on which each
Freeman had to strike his touch.

Treasury: A square inkstand, with
a lid: the name apparently deriving
from a type of inkwell used, in the
seventeenth century, at the Treasury
Office.

Treen: Vessels made from wood,
such as dishes and mugs. They
would at times be decorated with
or strengthened with pewter.

Triple-touch: A three-fold touch
found on Continental flatware.

Tryfill: Pewter of ordinary quality,
traditionally made up in part from
old pewter melted down. The name
is also spelt trifle.

Tundish: A funnel, specifically the
sort used in brewing to fit the
bung-hole of a barrel.

Vine and Grape: A form of
decoration representing a continuous vine tendril with bunches of
grapes and leaves, found on
Continental pewter.

Wriggled work: A traditional
form of English decoration,
consisting of a pattern made by
rocking a pointed tool against the
metal to form a series of dots.

X mark: Sometimes found
surmounted by a crown, this mark
was used in England to denote
'hard metal' ware or export quality,
and was a mark much imitated
abroad: in France, for example, a
XX mark is found denoting
superior quality.

York flagon: A traditional English
flagon shape with a bulbous shape
like an acorn-cup.

Typical beaker shapes:
1 North German beaker
2 Stop
3 French beaker
4 English beaker

Typical tankard shapes:
1 South German tankard
2 English tankard
3 Measuring tankard
4 Rörken
5 Arabesque tankard
6 Tankard with lid
7 Scottish tankard

148

Characteristically large mark
of the French pewterer
Antoine Fanon, working in
Lyons in the 18th century

Mark of Jean Petitot, Master
at Flavigny at the end of the
17th century

Proof mark used by the town
of Angers to stamp ware

Trademark for Tudric pewter,
manufactured for Liberty &
Co, London, by W.H. Haseler
in Birmingham. Tudric was
the major English brand of
Art Nouveau pewter

A display pewter mark, that
of Albrecht Preissensin, who
made the ornate dish
illustrated on the centre of
page 76

The mark of Jean Tardif,
pewterer at Angers in France
in 1716

The marks of Paul Beham, also known as Behem, Master of the Nuremberg pewterers in 1580, died 1610

Master at Lubeck, Johann Dahm made the unusual tobacco dish shown on page 48

Gottlob Friedrich Boeckmann was Master Pewterer in Tübingen, where he died in December 1874. He had succeeded to the business of his father, Peter Boeckmann

Quality marks, sometimes as found on pewter imported from England, by F. Doll

The device of an angel is common on German marks, and is seen here on that of Carl Georg Büttner

Ernst Dressler's touch shows the imaginative device of a shield within a shield

Marks of Johann Georg Bühler the Elder. A bottle by him is illustrated on page 34, left

George Drühl made the fine tankard with brassed thumbpiece seen on page 14

The Literature of Pewter

The intending collector's grasp of the subject can only be helped by reading and studying what others have written about pewter before him. The list of books that follows is by no means an exhaustive one, nor is it the suggestion that the collector should try and find room on his bookshelf for all the titles listed. But reference books can be a great help to the collector, and anyone contemplating starting a serious collection should bear in mind that books will be needed too. Even if the collector's own resources do not run to some of the more specialised and exotic titles listed, these can always be consulted in specialist libraries or museum reading rooms.

Another source of information is the art press. Though there is no specialist magazine in the United Kingdom on pewter, articles on the subject appear occasionally in magazines on art and antiques such as the *Antique Collector*, *Country Life*, *The Connoisseur* and so forth. Back issues of these magazines can be found in public libraries or museums.

A number of books on pewter are no longer in print, and must be sought in the second-hand market: here again there are a number of specialist bookshops, and art reference books are also sold at auction. The major London auction houses also sell pewter from time to time: as well as being a way of adding to one's collection, auction sales are normally well catalogued and the information in the catalogues can be of great use.

Antwerpen Tin

The catalogue of the Vleeshuis Museum collection of pewter, with 42 illustrations. Though in Dutch, it is a clear guide to pewter from Holland.

Sigrid Barten: Deutsches Jugendstijlzinn aus der Sammlung Hendrich

A catalogue of the German Art Nouveau pewter in the collection of the Art and Crafts Museum, Hamburg. Contains much information on Kayserzinn.

The bold design of Caspar Enderlein, Master in Nuremburg 1586

Born in 1729 in Altona, Nicolaus Essing practised his craft in Hamburg

The ornate lettering on Bernard Fahrenkrüger's mark is reflected in his designs, such as for the *Wilkomm* illustrated on page 50

Johann Adam Gwinner (1731 -1782) used the figure of justice for his mark

The nineteenth century marks of Johann Günzler, with a pewter proof mark

Quality marks used by Heinrich Hiller in the early 18th century

Marienburg was the centre of the Teutonic Order, thus Carl Hermersdörfer, used their imagery in his marks

HOLLAND
ORANIA
1373

Marks used by the important Art Nouveau pewterers Orania in Holland

Johann Höchel's mark shows the characteristic Jan Steen flagon shape, with his initials

The round and oval marks of the Kayser company, major manufacturers of Jugendstijl pewter

Howard H. Cotterell: Old Pewter, Its Makers and Marks

First published in 1929, now reprinted, this pioneering account of the history of English pewter contains a wealth of information on marks (including complete facsimiles of the pewter touchplates) and on the development of the London Guild. The book has 448 pages and 365 illustrations.

Howard H. Cotterell: Pewter Down the Ages

Though out of print for many years this book, published in 1932, is a good general guide to English and European pewter. It has a glossary, index and 159 illustrations.

Hans Demiani: Francòis Briot, Kaspar Enderlein und das Edelzinn

Published in Leipzig in 1897, this is still the best account of the French master and his German followers.

Ulrich Haedeke: Zinn

Published in Braunschweig in 1963, this is a useful handbook on German pewter, with 448 illustrations on 498 pages.

James Hatcher & P.C. Barker: A History of British Pewter

A thorough, modern account of British pewter, with particular reference to the seventeenth and eighteenth centuries. 386 pages with good illustrations.

Erwin Hintze: Die Deutschen Zinngiesser und ihre Marken

A seven volume study of German pewter, published in Leipzig between 1921 and 1926. The

Thomas Smith's mark (datable to 1761) shows the implements of a freemason: certain pewterers specialised in masonic ware.

John Appleton's mark contains a still and worm (or condensing pipe) for making alcohol.

This elegant mark, with the device of a phoenix, comes from the Exeter firm of Hall & Scott. The additional touch guaranteeing the quality of the metal is found on other makers' wares also.

Marks of Johann Matthias Timmermann the Elder, Master of the Hamburg Guild 1744. Died 1784.

Marks used by the Württembergische Metallwarenfabrik around the turn of the century.

Marx Wegmann, pewterer in Augsburg around 1620.

Touches of Christian Wolters, also of Hamburg. Master in 1751, he died about twenty years later.

books list and illustrate over 4,400 marks.

H.J.L.J. Massé: The Pewter Collector

'A Guide to British pewter, with some reference to foreign work' was the original subtitle of this book, first published in 1921 and revised by R.F. Michaelis in 1971. The book contains a glossary, a complete list of pewterers' names and an index to the touchplates with drawings of marks, as well as a general introduction to the subject and several illustrations.

Ronald Michaelis: British Pewter

This introductory book has a brief text matched by 40 or so well-chosen pictures.

Charles F. Montgomery: A History of American Pewter

A good account of pewter in the USA, which discusses history and technique with plentiful illustrations. This book has 264 pages and was published in 1974.

C.H. Peal: British Pewter and Britannia Metal

This book, with 192 pages, partly illustrated in colour, is one of the few to deal seriously with Britannia metal for collectors.

C.H. Peal: More Pewter Marks

This new book makes available a considerable body of newly found and unpublished marks.

Marks of Gottlieb Kare, who made the neoclassical candlestick shown on page 40

An early German mark, that of Jacob Koch, Master of the Nuremburg Pewterers in 1583

Marks used by the pewterer Gottlieb Kraeft. Either for ware imported from England or for ware made to the English standards

London & X marks found on pewter for export or to export standard

Marks of the brothers Hans and Peter Krafft

Marks of Jürgen Lütkens, maker of the brassed and ornate tankard seen on the left on page 66

Hermann Daniel Meyer, Lubeck, who made the *Wilkomm* shown on the bottom of page 46

The crossed anchor mark of Carl Noster (or Nuster) who died in 1841

„ORIVIT"
2216

Mark of the Orivit company, makers of Art Nouveau pewter in Cologne

Tardy: Les Etains Français

This large book illustrates a wealth of examples of French pewter, with notes on maker and date.

Tardy: Les Poincons d'Etain

A pocket guide to pewter marks from all over the world, though the main emphasis is on French marks. The book is particularly useful to the collector of European ware.

Kenneth Ullyett: Pewter - A Guide for Collectors

As well as a glossary and index, this book contains a list of recorded touches. It also has a good introductory section on pewter in North America.

L. Ingleby Wood: Scottish Pewterware

This book is long out of print, but it does contain a full account of the history of pewter in Scotland, and illustrations of the pewter touch-plates preserved in Edinburgh.

Charles Welch: History of the Worshipful Company of Pewterers

This very full account of the guild was first published in 1902, in two volumes. A briefer history of the Company was published by Ronald Michaelis in 1972, and this also includes a catalogue of the pewter in the Company's collection.

Pewter in Museums

The pewter collector can look for guidance to several sources when building up his collection. One of the most important sources, apart from the written sources already mentioned, is the collection of works preserved in museums and art galleries.

In that pewter was in widespread use until fairly recently, most local or civic museums will have some examples on display or in store, and, particularly where there was a local pewter industry, it is always worth a collector's while to get to know the curators and staff of a local musuem, who often have knowledge they are happy to share. Likewise, any reputable antique dealer should be happy to offer his opinion on an item, though dealers who specialize in pewter are few. The major auction houses will also offer an 'on the spot' valuation of any item brought into their rooms.

The following museums have considerable collections of pewter, and are worth a visit. The *Victoria and Albert Museum*, South Kensington, London has a department of metalwork and a display, as does the *London Museum*, London Wall. The *City Museum* at St. Albans has a collection of Roman pewter, as does the museum at Lincoln. In France there are collections in the *Musée des Beaux* Arts in Strasbourg. Mention should also be made of the pewter in the *Tiroler Landesmuseum* in Innsbruck and the *Österreichisches Museum für angewandte Kunst* in Vienna. In West Germany there are collections in Frankfurt, Hamburg (both the Art and Crafts Museum and the Hamburg Museum) Munich, Nuremburg and Cologne. Swiss pewter, with its many distinctive shapes, can be found in museums in Zurich.

Index

Photograph acknowledgements:

Christie, Manson and Woods, London

Museum fur Hamburgische Geschichte, Hamburg

Weygang Museum, Öhringen

Münchner Kunstauktionshaus KG Neumeister, Munich

Galerie Decorative Arts, Kenneth Barlow, Munich

Sammlung Ferdinand Nees, Munich

Galerie XX Wolfgang Uecker, Hamburg

Sammlung Hartz, Hamburg

Antiquitäten Marita Meyer, Hamburg

Die Nue Sammlung, Staatliches Museum für angewandte Kunst, Munich

Photographers:

Jacques Hartz, Hamburg
Neumeister KG, Munich
Johann Rosenhagen, Ohringen
Special thanks are offered to Herr Johann Rosenhagen of the Weygang Museum, Ohringen, who gave such valuable help.